S.P.C.K. THEOLOGICAL COLLECTIONS

The Christian Hope

THEOLOGICAL COLLECTIONS

13

THE CHRISTIAN HOPE

G. B. Caird

Wolfhart Pannenberg

I. T. Ramsey

James Klugmann

Ninian Smart

W. A. Whitehouse

LONDON

S · P · C · K

1970

First published in 1970
by S.P.C.K.
Holy Trinity Church
Marylebone Road
London N.W.1

Printed in Great Britain by
The Talbot Press (S.P.C.K.)
Saffron Walden Essex

SBN 281 02352 2

CONTENTS

PUBLISHER'S NOTE

This volume of THEOLOGICAL COLLECTIONS contains versions (revised in certain cases) of papers delivered at the annual conference of the Society for the Study of Theology, held at Lake Hall in the University of Birmingham 25-28 March 1969. The paper by the Bishop of Durham is his Presidential Address. A paper on "The Case for Universalism", delivered at this conference by the Reverend Professor John Hick, is not included within this collection since it forms part of a larger volume of his essays to be published in due course by the University Press of Virginia and Macmillan and Company Limited.

NOTES ON CONTRIBUTORS

The Reverend Dr G. B. Caird is Senior Tutor of Mansfield College, Oxford.

Dr Wolfhart Pannenberg is a member of the Protestant Theological faculty and Director of the Ecumenical Institute of the University of Munich.

The Right Reverend Dr I. T. Ramsey is Bishop of Durham and was President of the Society for the Study of Theology for 1968—1969.

Mr James Klugmann is Editor of *Marxism Today*.

Mr Ninian Smart is Professor of Religious Studies in the University of Lancaster.

The Reverend W. A. Whitehouse is Professor of Theology in the University of Kent at Canterbury.

ACKNOWLEDGEMENTS

Thanks are due to the following for permission to quote from copyright sources:

The Aristotelian Society: an article by W. C. Kneale in *Proceedings of the Aristotelian Society* (1960-1).

Central Books Ltd: *How Steel was Tempered*, by Nikolai Ostrovsky

Collins Publishers: *From Primitives to Zen*, by Mircea Eliade.

The Congregational Church in England and Wales: *A Declaration of Faith adopted by the Congregational Church of England and Wales.*

Ecumenical Review and Professor Jean Meyendorff: "The Significance of the Reformation in the History of Christendom" (vol. xvi, January 1964).

Epworth Press and the Fortress Press: *Christian Theology and Metaphysics*, by Peter Baelz.

Oxford University Press and the University of Durham: *Christianity in an Age of Science*, by C. A. Coulson.

Quotations from *The New English Bible, New Testament* (1961) are by permission of Oxford and Cambridge University Presses.

I

THE CHRISTOLOGICAL BASIS OF CHRISTIAN HOPE

G. B. CAIRD

Christians, said Paul, should not grieve for their dead "like the rest of men, who have no hope" (1 Thess. 4. 13). At first blush this might seem to be an ungenerous, not to say an ill-informed, estimate of non-Christian religion. Surely the prevailing gloom of the first century, so well attested by its epitaphs, ought not to have made Paul forget that many Jews believed in the resurrection of the just and many Gentiles in the immortality of the soul, or in an escape from mortality by initiation into one of the numerous mystery cults. If we look beyond Paul's immediate environment to the whole history of religion, then from many parts of the world and from many periods of history comes ample evidence that God has put eternity into man's heart and given him "immortal longings". Nevertheless, Paul's claim that the Christian alone has hope can be defended, if we make a proper distinction between hope and desire. The *Oxford English Dictionary* defines hope as "desire combined with expectation". The word has, to be sure, like its counterparts in other languages, often been used to denote either a baseless optimism ("He that lives upon hope will die fasting") or a vague yearning after unattainable good ("Hope sows what Love shall never reap"). But if hope is to be genuine hope, it must be founded on something which affords reasonable grounds for confidence in its fulfilment. It must have a basis.

The ostensible basis for Christian hope in the New Testament is the resurrection of Christ. "God not only raised our Lord from the dead; he will also raise us by his power (1 Cor. 6. 14; cf. 15. 12-20; 2 Cor. 4. 14; Rom. 8. 11). "Praise be to the God and Father of our Lord Jesus Christ, who in his mercy gave us new birth into a living hope by the resurrection of Jesus Christ from the dead" (1 Pet. 1. 3). "To the Conqueror I will grant a seat beside me on my throne, as I myself conquered and sat down beside my Father on his throne" (Rev. 3. 21). "Because I live, you too will live" (John 14. 19). It is no

9

part of my purpose to cast doubt on this central affirmation of the Christian faith. I hold that the historical evidence both for the resurrection appearances and for the empty tomb is earlier and more reliable than sceptics, outside or inside of the Church, have been ready to allow. But on one point I agree with the sceptics, that this evidence *by itself* proves very little. Such criticism has commonly been directed against the accounts of the empty tomb. "Let us suppose", wrote Maurice Goguel, "that a document was found which established beyond cavil that on the morning of the third day the tomb of Jesus was found empty. Let us suppose that the demonstrative evidence was accepted by all historians. Do you imagine it would be enough to convert them to the Christian faith?"[1] To this I would add that the same must be said of the resurrection appearances. Let us suppose that tomorrow you were confronted with irrefutable evidence that an acquaintance whom you had good reason to believe dead had been seen alive by reliable witnesses. You would certainly feel compelled to revise some of your ideas about science, but I doubt whether you would feel compelled to revise your ideas about God. I doubt whether you would conclude that your acquaintance was divine, or that a stamp of authenticity had been placed on all he ever said or did, or even that he would not yet, at some time in the future, have to die.

Why then did the first Christians find the evidence of the appearances and the empty tomb so convincing and so full of far-reaching implications? As Jews, no doubt, they believed in a general resurrection at the Last Day (cf. John 11. 24), but that would have given them no grounds whatever for believing in the resurrection of one man while history continued to run its course otherwise undisturbed. Whatever we may make of the resurrection predictions recorded in the Gospels, they must not be allowed to detract from the clear evidence that the resurrection, when it happened, took the disciples wholly by surprise. Before long, admittedly, they were claiming that the resurrection had taken place "according to the Scriptures"; but those Scriptures are neither so numerous nor so obvious as to provide the source of the Easter faith. What is even more important is that the early Christians were themselves aware of these difficulties. The Lucan and Matthaean accounts of the resurrection reflect a variety of doubts which must have been felt inside as well as outside of the Church, and the parable of Dives and Lazarus ends with a warning that the world is not likely to be convinced merely by the return of a man from the

---

[1] "Le caractère de la foi à la résurrection dans le christianisme primitif", *Revue d'histoire et de philosophie religieuses* (1931), pp. 335f.

grave (Luke 16. 31). Why then did they believe? The answer must lie in their experience of the earthly Jesus; there was something about his earthly life which made the resurrection, once it had happened, seem the natural, proper, and convincing sequel. This, as I hope to show, is the general consensus of the New Testament. "God raised him to life again, setting him free from the pangs of death, because it could not be that death should keep him in its grip" (Acts 2. 24). "He owes his priesthood not to a system of earth-bound rules, but to the power of an indestructible life" (Heb. 7. 16). "The prince of this world is coming, but he has no hold over me" (John 14. 30).

The orthodox Christian, who has been taught to believe in the divinity of Christ, may feel it to be self-evident that death could not hold him. But this short cut is not open to us. Granted that the speed with which the early Church came to accord divine honours to Jesus of Nazareth is one of the most impressive facts of New Testament theology, it would nevertheless be rash to maintain that belief in the incarnation antedated and provided a warrant for belief in the resurrection; and it would also be fatal to our present enterprise. A Jesus who rose from the dead because he was divine would furnish no basis of hope that mortal men too might escape the pangs of death. The basis for that hope must be sought where I believe the early Church found it—in the humanity of Jesus.

AN INDESTRUCTIBLE LIFE

The first part of my thesis then is that the disciples of Jesus found the evidence for the resurrection credible because of some quality they had observed in the human conduct and experience of Jesus; and of this I propose to give four examples.

1. I have already quoted the verse from Peter's Pentecost speech which declares that death could not hold Jesus. The reason for this is given in an extended quotation from Psalm 16:

> I foresaw that Lord's presence would always be with me;
> He is at my right hand, and so I cannot be shaken.
> Therefore my heart is glad and my tongue exults,
> Yes, and my body shall dwell in hope.
> For you will not abandon my life to the grave
> Or let your loyal one suffer corruption.
> You have shown me the paths of life
> And will fill me with gladness in your presence.
>
> (Acts 2. 25-8)

In the commentary on this psalm which follows, Peter argues that,

although David was the author, he cannot be the "I" of the psalm, since he in fact died and was buried. He was writing prophetically, putting himself in the place of his descendant, the Messiah. The Messiah, though a human, mortal king of David's lineage, would be delivered from death because his whole life would be lived in the presence of God, and that presence alone would be his guarantee of ultimate felicity. To live continually in the presence of God is to tread the paths of life.

2. There is nothing in the epistles of Paul comparable to this, except the two passages where he speaks of the obedience of Jesus. "As through the disobedience of the one man the many were made sinners, so through the obedience of the one man the many will be made righteous" (Rom. 5. 19). "He assumed the nature of a slave and was born like other men. Appearing in human form, he humbled himself and was obedient to the point of death, even death on a cross. Therefore God raised him high" (Phil. 2. 7-9). The second of these passages clearly asserts that the exaltation of Jesus was the consequence of his lifelong obedience. We must be careful, however, not to allow a residual legalism to distort Paul's meaning. He is not saying that man, having failed to satisfy the demands of God by his own merits, can satisfy them vicariously by sharing in the merits of Christ. The obedience of Christ is held up as an example for believers to follow, and, so hotly and constantly does Paul repudiate the idea that man's standing with God depends on merit, that we are bound to conclude that this is true even of Christ. He too must have lived by grace and grace alone. His obedience was offered not to the demands of law but to the demands of love. It was a willing participation in the divine purpose of redemption. Thus Paul too believed that the human life of Jesus was lived in close communion with God. It had always been the purpose of God that man should live face to face with the divine perfection and reflect it in his own character; and the disastrous consequence of sin was that it removed man from the divine presence and so cut him off from the source of the glory he was designed to bear—"all have sinned and lost the glory of God" (Rom. 3. 23). This glory had been restored in Jesus, not only in the splendour of his risen power (2 Cor. 4. 6), but also in the incognito of his earthly obedience (1 Cor. 2. 8).

3. This theme receives much fuller treatment in the Epistle to the Hebrews. The main argument of the epistle is that the Old Testament is not only an incomplete book, but a book aware of its own incompleteness, full of warnings to the reader not to make himself at home in it or find in it his abiding city. One of the inadequacies of

the old regime of the law, with its system of priesthood and sacrifice, is that it had not the power to lead its adherents to their destined perfection. "The law contains but a shadow . . . of the good things which were to come; it provides for the same sacrifices year after year, and with these it can never bring the worshippers to perfection for all time" (10.1; cf. 7. 11; 8. 19; 9. 9). Perfection in this epistle clearly has some moral content, but it is not to be identified simply with moral goodness. For three times we are told that Christ himself, "dedicated, innocent, undefiled, separated" as he was (7. 26), still had to become perfect. "It was fitting that God, the goal and source of all that is, in bringing many sons to glory, should make the pioneer of their salvation perfect through suffering" (2. 10). "In the days of his earthly life he offered up prayers and petitions, with loud cries and tears, to God who was able to save him from death; and in the midst of his fear his prayer was heard. Son though he was, he learned obedience in the school of suffering, and, once perfected, became the source of eternal salvation to all who obey him" (5. 7-9). "The priest appointed by the oath which supersedes the law is the Son, made perfect for ever" (7. 28). The meaning which lies on the surface of all three passages is that, if Christ was to be the pioneer of man's salvation, he must be like them in every respect, exhausting all the possibilities of human temptation and suffering, following to its end the path of obedience to God. By this means he was "made perfect", that is, fully qualified for his task. But underlying this is an even more important idea. If Christ is to be the pioneer, he must open up a new road which others will be able to follow. He must therefore have no powers at his disposal which are not also available to them. "He who consecrates and they who are consecrated are all of one" (2. 11). They are derived from one stock and must draw their sanctity from the one source, which is God. Hence the author puts into the mouth of Jesus the words of Isaiah : "I will keep my trust fixed on him." Like his followers, Jesus must live by faith and prayer, discovering by personal experience what it means to be utterly obedient to God, and, even in face of the terrors of Gethsemane, leaving the results in the hands of God.

Along with the theme of perfection goes the theme of access. "Nothing was brought to perfection by the law, but by the introduction of a better hope, by which we draw near to God" (7. 19; cf. 4. 14-16; 7. 25; 10. 1, 22; 12. 18, 22). Man reaches perfection only through standing in the presence of God. The old covenant failed because it taught that only the morally fit may enter the divine presence; and so the way to God was barricaded as long as the old system lasted. The new covenant teaches that God is himself the only source of moral fitness and offers open access to God on the

grounds of faith alone. But the corollary of this is that Jesus himself
must have derived his goodness from the divine presence. The
right of approach to the throne of grace carries with it all that men
can hope or desire, including both holiness and eternal life. Eternal
life does not consist in living for ever, but in living with God.

4. The Fourth Gospel might appear to be unpromising territory for
our investigation, for the commonly held opinion has been that the
evangelist barely discriminates between the pre-existent Logos, the
historical Jesus, and the glorified Christ. It is the outstanding merit
of the work of W. H. Cadman[2] that he has questioned this long-
accepted dogma of criticism and has offered us an alternative, which
is at once more attractive and more probable; and in what now
follows I am indebted to him. John never uses the title "Son" of the
pre-existent Logos, but only of the incarnate Logos, the man Jesus.
It is accordingly the historical Jesus who is said to be "in the bosom
of the Father" (NEB—"nearest to the Father's heart"). When Jesus
declares that "no one ever ascended to heaven except the one who
descended from heaven, the Son of Man who is in heaven", he is
not the glorified Christ speaking literally about what we call the
Ascension, but the earthly Jesus speaking figuratively about the communion with God which he already enjoyed at the moment when
he was conversing with Nicodemus (3. 13). Similarly, when he claims
to speak only what he has seen or heard from his Father (3. 11, 31-2;
8. 26, 28, 38, 47; 12. 49; 14. 10), this is not to be construed as
memory of a precosmic existence as Logos, from which he has
come into the world "trailing clouds of glory". His whole earthly
life has been a continuous process of watching and listening to his
Father. The clearest evidence for this is found in the parable of the
Apprenticed Son. "A son can do nothing by himself; he does only
what he sees his father doing: what the father does, the son does.
For the father loves his son and shows him all that he is doing"
(5. 19-20). Here we have a picture of a human father instructing his
son in his own trade and sharing with him all his professional
secrets, and through the lens of this picture from daily life we are to
see the relation between Jesus and God. So complete is the mutual
understanding of this partnership that everything Jesus says or
does is at the same time the word or deed of God. It is a partnership
of mutual love (15. 9-10) and mutual indwelling (10. 38; 14. 11). On
the side of Jesus it is characterized by humility, obedience, and
total dependence; yet so totally is his person laid at the disposal
of the Father's purpose that the divine truth, light, and glory can
be manifested through him to the world. The important point for

2 *The Open Heaven.*

our study is that all this applies also to Jesus' possession of eternal life. "As the Father has life in himself, so also he has granted to the Son to have life in himself" (5. 26). For Jesus, as later for his disciples, eternal life is not the sequel to bodily death, nor is it a matter of endless duration, a prospect which most people in any case have found daunting. It is a quality of existence derived from communion with God, from the fact that he is in the Father and the Father in him.

It was one of the weaknesses of the older, dogmatic approach to the gospel that it could provide no reasonable explanation for the descent of the Spirit on Jesus. Why should the incarnate Logos need in addition the power and guidance of the Spirit? It is absurd to suggest that John has included this episode, without attempting to incorporate it into his own theology, simply because it came to him in the tradition. He omitted too many important elements of the tradition for that to be plausible, including the Transfiguration, the Institution of the Lord's Supper, and, above all, the Baptism, to which the descent of the Spirit was traditionally an adjunct. There must be a theological explanation, and Cadman can offer us one. In the farewell discourse the disciples are told that the crucifixion will establish an objective union between Christ and themselves, but that they will have to await the coming of the Paraclete, the Spirit of truth, before they can enter into a subjective apprehension of what has happened. In the same way the incarnation established an objective union between the Logos and the individual manhood of Jesus. But the man Jesus needed the guidance of the Spirit to lead him to a subjective awareness of this fact. He had to attain, in the reality of religious experience, to a knowledge of God, which in his case was at the same time self-knowledge. It was true of him, as later of his disciples, that only when he came to see himself as he truly was did he also see the Father.

These four very different writers are thus in agreement about the one central affirmation: that the man Jesus already possessed during his earthly career a life over which death had no power, an indestructible, eternal life, because he lived in such close union with God that, without any loss of identity, his human personality was taken up into the divine. To their testimony we may now add that of the Synoptic teaching of Jesus. In answer to a tendentious question from the Sadducees about levirate marriage and the afterlife Jesus replies that life after death is a scriptural doctrine. "Now about the resurrection of the dead, have you never read in the Book of Moses, in the story of the burning bush, how God spoke to him and said, 'I am the God of Abraham, the God of Isaac, and the God of Jacob'?

God is not the God of the dead but of the living" (Mark 12. 26-7). This is not to be dismissed as a clever *ad hominem* argument. It is a profound theological assertion that

> Life, like a fountain rich and free,
> Springs from the presence of the Lord.

In one of the papers read to the Fiftieth Annual Conference of Modern Churchmen, P. N. Hamilton made an interesting experiment in expressing Christology in modern terms by use of Whitehead's "theory of prehensions". "It attempts to describe the manner in which one entity is actually, not just metaphorically, immanent in another—actually immanent in that it contributes to and is constituent in the other's subjectivity." Hamilton illustrated this theory from the experience of husband and wife of growing together until each "becomes partially and objectively immanent in the other". He concluded: "Thus the belief that God's self-expressive activity was supremely present in the person and the decision of the historical Jesus implies the belief that Jesus was supremely *sympatique* to God, and that God is supremely compatible to Jesus."[3] I am not qualified to discuss the claims of process philosophy to be an adequate vehicle for a new Christology, nor do I profess to understand in what way a metaphorical immanence would differ from an actual one. Such matters I am content to leave to the philosopher and the systematic theologian. But I thought it worth mentioning that Hamilton seems to me to be looking for new terms to say what is already said in a variety of ways in the New Testament.

A LIVING HOPE

So far I have been trying to determine what it was that caused the early Christians to accept the reports of the empty grave and the appearances as convincing evidence that Jesus was "alive for evermore". But this in itself gave them no grounds for the further affirmation that he held "the keys of death and the grave". To say that his possession of eternal life depended on the closeness of his communion with God might have seemed, on the contrary, to put eternal life for ever beyond the grasp of those who knew themselves to be unable to bear comparison with him and to be debarred by sin from the divine presence. Yet the early Christians never drew this depressing conclusion. From the beginning they regarded the resurrection not only as a sign that Christ was alive, but as a

---

[3] "Some Proposals for a Modern Christology", in *Christ for us Today*, ed. N. Pittenger, pp. 162f.

guarantee that they would live also. To find the basis for this hope we must return to the evidence and scrutinize it more thoroughly.

1. My first illustration was from the Pentecost speech of Peter. We must now take cognizance of the fact that the proof of the credibility of the resurrection was there found in a quotation from Scripture. The idea that the life, death, and resurrection of Jesus took place "according to the Scriptures" is not of course peculiar to the Lucan writings, but in them it has a peculiar theological purport. The Old Testament is cited to show that all things have happened "by the deliberate plan and foreknowledge of God" (Acts 2. 23). In the Gospel, too, Luke makes frequent use of the verb δεῖ to show that the whole ministry of Jesus was controlled by a divine and scriptural necessity. On the other hand, it has been frequently re- marked that the speeches in Acts assign no atoning significance to the cross, and the inference used to be drawn that this was no part of the most primitive kerygma, but had been introduced into it by Paul. There are two good reasons for rejecting this specious con- clusion. Paul explicitly states that "he died for our sins according to the scriptures" was part of the tradition he had received (1 Cor. 15. 3), and in his Gospel Luke omits the two Marcan sayings which interpret the cross as a ransom or a covenant sacrifice (Mark 10. 45; 14. 24). Though he is the only evangelist to quote Isaiah 53 in the Passion narrative, the verse he quotes ("He was numbered with the outlaws") says nothing of the Servant as scapegoat or sin-offering. It is likely therefore that the omission of the atoning death from the speeches in Acts is also due to the editorial activity of Luke. How then are we to account for this apparent contradiction, that Luke plays down the atoning effect of the cross, but that he insists that it happened in accordance with the plan of God? The obvious answer is that Luke believed that the atoning work of Christ ought not to be concentrated on Calvary. From the moment of the Annunciation it could be said that God had "visited and redeemed his people" (1. 68). The whole ministry of Jesus was the promised coming or visit of God (7. 16; 19. 44). Jesus could bring salvation "today" to the house of Zacchaeus, because he carried with him the saving presence of God (19. 9). If at the end he was crucified between two criminals, it was because he had all along chosen to be numbered with the outlaws. The cross was the price he had to pay for being the friend of outcasts and sinners and for making their cause his own. But even this friendship could not have been a saving friendship if it had not embodied and been prompted by the eternal plan of God. Our study of Luke's theology began with Jesus living constantly in the presence of the Lord. But this was no static or contemplative union; it was a

sharing of God's purpose and love for mankind. "Everything is entrusted to me by my Father; and no one knows who the Son is but the Father, or who the Father is but the Son, and those to whom the Son may choose to reveal him" (10. 22). By the gracious will of God he had been enabled to identify himself fully with the divine purpose, but that purpose required of him an equally thoroughgoing identification with men. His friendship with God is his own guarantee of eternal life. His friendship with men is the means by which they too are introduced into the same immortalizing presence.

2. For this second part of our theme Pauline illustrations are not far to seek. No New Testament writer goes to greater lengths to emphasize the total identification of Jesus with mankind. "Christ was innocent of sin, and yet for our sake God made him one with the sinfulness of men" (2 Cor. 5. 21). "Christ bought us freedom from the curse of the law by becoming for our sake an accursed thing" (Gal. 3. 13). "God sent his own Son in a form like that of our own sinful nature, and for sin" (Rom. 8. 3). "He loved me and gave himself for me" (Gal. 2. 20). The most striking expression of this conviction is found in the so-called christological hymn in Philippians, which provided the main Pauline evidence for the relation of Jesus to God. "He assumed the nature of a slave." The order of the clauses rules out the possibility that Paul is thinking of Jesus as Servant of the Lord. The servile form was what he assumed at the incarnation, not a role he chose to fulfil during his earthly ministry. In becoming man he accepted servitude to all the varied powers of evil which haunted the individual and corporate life of humanity and, by constant obedience to God, broke their control over himself and others. Paul's whole doctrine of redemption may be summed up in a single sentence: Christ identified himself with men in their sin, helplessness, and defeat, in order that they might be identified with him in his victory, power, and holiness. But in his theology, as in that of Luke, it is presupposed that his actions were prompted by the indwelling grace and love of God. Indeed, Paul regularly makes God the subject of his christological or soteriological statements. It was God who sent his Son (Gal. 4. 4; Rom. 8. 3), God who in Christ was working out man's salvation (2 Cor. 5. 19; Col. 2. 9), God who delivered him up to death (Rom. 3. 25; 4. 25) and raised him to glory (Rom. 6. 4; 1 Cor. 15. 15; 2 Cor. 4. 14; Gal. 1. 1; Phil. 2. 9). When Christ died, it was God who was commending his own love to sinners (Rom. 5. 8). Even when he is more deeply sensitive to the burden of mortality, Paul can declare himself more than conqueror, because he knows that nothing can separate him from the love of God in Christ Jesus (Rom. 8. 18-39). Whether Christians sleep or

wake, they will be alive with Christ (1 Thess. 5. 10), for to be alive is to be within the sustaining love of God. "In dying as he died, he died to sin, once for all, and in living as he lives, he lives to God. In the same way you must regard yourselves as dead to sin and alive to God, in union with Christ Jesus" (Rom. 6. 10-11). For Paul life, here or hereafter, means being "alive to God".

3. In the rest of the New Testament there is nothing that exactly corresponds to Paul's simile or metaphor of the body. But the idea of corporate solidarity can be just as real and as vivid when it is expressed in terms of personal relationship, and those terms have the added advantage of not being liable to literalistic misinterpretation. We have already seen that in Hebrews the perfecting of Christ required that he should undergo the whole range of human temptation and suffering. The purpose of this is not only to ensure that he was fully human, but also that he was fully qualified by personal experience to sympathize with the ignorance and error of others (2. 17-18; 5. 2). Because of this experience he "does not shrink from calling men his brothers" (2. 12); they are "the children whom God has given me" (2. 13), and he "takes them to himself (2. 16). The whole elaborate argument about Aaron and Melchizedek turns on the duty of the high priest to be men's representative before God (5. 1).

Writers who ought to have known better have made unfavourable comparisons between this epistle and Paul or the Fourth Gospel, on the ground that here the atoning work of Christ is not grounded in the love of God. It is true that the word *agape* is not used, except twice to denote a Christian virtue (6. 10; 10. 24). But let us not be slaves to the concordance. The theology of this epistle could very well be entitled "Atonement by Sympathy"; and the sufferings of Christ which qualified him to be the sympathetic high priest are said to have had their source in the character of God. "It befitted God . . . in bringing many sons to glory, to make the pioneer of their salvation perfect through suffering" (2.10). But there is a later passage which gives more eloquent expression to this belief. In presenting the death of Christ as the sacrifice to end all sacrifice, our author quotes from the LXX version of Psalm 40. 6-8 :

> Sacrifice and offering you do not desire,
> But you have prepared a body for me.
> In whole-offerings and sin-offerings you take no pleasure.
> Then I said, "Here I am : as it is written of me in the scroll,
> I have come to do your will, God."

On this he makes the illuminating comment that "it is by this will that we have been made holy". Christ's death is efficacious, not simply because he identified himself with his brothers, but because it was God's will that he should do so. Because Christ lived and died "in that will", he could be "a new priest . . . owing his priesthood . . . to the power of an indestructible life", and could stand for "the introduction of a better hope, through which we draw near to God" (7. 16-19).

4. We have already seen that in the Fourth Gospel the earthly Jesus is said to be "in the bosom of the Father". His whole life is spent in watching and listening to his Father and in doing his work, or rather, in allowing the Father to work through him. "It is the Father who dwells in me doing his own work" (14. 10). But what is this work of God? There are eminent scholars who have thought it to be nothing more than a work of revelation, leaving no place for the kind of identification of Christ with men which we have found elsewhere. If we were to restrict ourselves to the first half of the Gospel, this verdict might stand, though even there we find many hints that it is not the whole story. In the first twelve chapters Jesus is a lonely figure, the only Son who goes where others cannot follow him, demonstrating in every act his unique relationship to God. His relationship to men is concentrated wholly in the Passion. We are told, certainly, that he has loved his disciples all along; but it is only when he loves them to the uttermost that they are enabled to "have part with him" (13. 8), only then that he goes to prepare a place for them, so that they may be where he is—in the bosom of the Father (14. 2). "I, if I am lifted up from the earth, will draw all men to me" (12. 32). At this point in the Gospel all the terms which have been used to describe the unique interrelationship of Father and Son are put to new service in describing the analogous relationship of Jesus and believers: glory and love, life and truth, abiding and sending, mutual indwelling and mutual knowledge. It hardly needs to be added that all this issues from the love of God for the world (3. 16), which Jesus shares, and of which he has become the perfect mediator. Into the eternal love which subsists between God and the Logos is taken up first the individual manhood of Jesus, then those who by the cross are drawn into his inclusive manhood, then those who believe through their testimony, and finally the world.

To all this it may be objected that I have paid far too little attention to the incarnation, especially since three of the writers whom I have put in the witness-box undoubtedly believed in the pre-existence of Christ. I can only answer that this would have carried me beyond my brief. It does not appear to me that the

Christian hope, as it is set forth in the New Testament, rests in any obvious sense on the pre-existence of Christ. The hope of eternal life rests rather on the conviction that the man Jesus enjoyed so close a relationship to God that death could not be more than a brief interruption of it; and on the confidence that, because he has established a similarly close relationship with men, he has opened up to them the possibility of sharing his life in God's presence.

THE NEW HEAVEN AND EARTH

There has been, however, one considerable omission, which I must now endeavour to make good. Up to this point I have been assuming that the content of the Christian hope is the life everlasting. I do not want in any way to retract this. Paul speaks for the New Testament as a whole when he says that, "if it is for this life only that Christ has given us hope, we of all men are most to be pitied" (1 Cor. 15. 19). But the question we must now face is whether we are not equally deluded if our hope is entirely in the world to come. Too often evangelical Christianity has treated the souls of men as brands plucked from the burning and the world in general as a grim vale of soul-making. It has been content to see the splendour of the created universe, together with all the brilliant achievements of human labour, skill, and thought, as nothing more than the expendable backdrop for the drama of redemption. One of the reasons why men of our generation have turned against conventional Christianity is that they think it involves writing off the solid joys of this present life for the doubtful acquisition of some less substantial treasure. We ought to take their views very seriously, for they were shared by the Hebrews of the Old Testament. Most of the books of the Old Testament were written at a time when the Hebrew people had no belief in an afterlife for the individual. For them life meant this life. Like the God of their creation story, they looked at the world, and behold, it was very good. Their eschatology was concerned with the vindication in history of the truth and justice of God and of his purpose for Israel and the world. The end they looked for might be described as a new heaven and a new earth but this was figurative language, and what they meant was the present heaven and earth renewed by the transfiguring radiance of God. When they developed a belief in an afterlife for the individual, it was grafted somewhat uneasily on to the older and more earthly hope. A large part of our difficulty with New Testament eschatology is caused by our attempts to force it into an alien dogmatic mould. I can, for example, think of no passage in the New Testament which promises that we shall go to heaven when we die. It is true that our inheritance

or treasure or new life is frequently said to be laid up for us in heaven; but a man who inherits a fortune does not have to live in the vaults of his father's bank in order to enjoy it. The whole point of the resurrection of the body is that the life of the world to come is to be lived on a renewed earth. We do Paul a grave injustice if we dismiss his talk about the emancipation of the physical universe from its bondage to futility and corruption as a mere flight of poetic fancy. He had a view of the relation of man to his cosmic environment which is quite astonishingly modern. Man is part and parcel of the created order and must be saved in his integrity, or he is not really saved at all.

It would be possible to spend a long time enlarging on this theme; but the question to which we must address ourselves is this: Did the person and work of Christ provide any secure basis for such a hope as this? There are two lines of thought which we could pursue in an attempt to answer this question out of the New Testament. We could return to our starting-point and argue that, although the reports of the appearances and the empty tomb were not convincing independently of the impression Jesus had already made on his disciples, nevertheless, once accepted, they were rapidly built into the structure of theology and regarded as indications of the conquest of death and the ultimate emancipation of the world from its control. I prefer to follow the second line, which at least has the merit of being consistent with the rest of this paper. I have argued that Jesus himself possessed eternal life and made it available to others in virtue of his perfect humanity, that is, because he enjoyed a communion with God for which man in God's image had always been destined. But man made in God's image had also been destined to exercise dominion over the rest of God's works. I believe it can be demonstrated that Paul's whole doctrine of the end, and his vision of a universe redeemed, whatever minor factors may have contributed to it, is in the main a logical development of his belief in Christ as man in God's image. He started of course from the commonly accepted idea of his own day that the subhuman creation had been involved in the fall of man; the ground had been cursed for his sake and, deprived of proper control, nature had become red in tooth and claw. But Paul was never tied to any merely literalistic interpretation of Old Testament myth. He did not need to believe that there ever was a time when Adam actually exercised that dominion over all creation which he now attributed to Christ. All he needed to believe was that God had deliberately left his creation incomplete, in order that it might be completed by the co-operation of man, and that with the coming of Christ this co-operation had become a genuine possibility. And in fact he makes it quite plain that

the first Adam, who was merely ψύχικος (endowed with natural
life) could never have fulfilled the functions of the last Adam, who
was πνευμάτικος (endowed with spiritual life).

I must leave it to others to explore the meaning of this vision for
modern theology. Let me end by placing alongside of it two other
visions from the New Testament. The first comes at the conclusion
of the contrast between Mount Sinai and Mount Sion in Hebrews.
"God has promised, 'Yet once again I will shake not earth alone, but
the heavens also.' The words 'once again'—and only once—imply
that the shaking of these created things means their removal, and
then what is not shaken will remain. The kingdom we are given is
unshakable; let us therefore give thanks to God, and so worship
him as he would be worshipped, with reverence and awe; for our
God is a consuming fire" (Heb. 12. 26-9). The great earthquake and
the devouring fire are such familiar symbols of the divine judgement
that it is easy to miss the new twist that is here being given to them.
Here is no Platonic contrast between the phenomenal, earthly, and
transient on the one hand and the noumenal, heavenly, and permanent on the other. The author believes that he and his friends,
transient creatures that they are, have been given a share in the
realm of the unshakable. The difference between the shakable and
the unshakable, then, lies not in their natural status, but in their
relationship to God. There is much in this world that deserves to be
removed by the earthquake of God's displeasure or consumed in the
fire of his holiness. But whatever gains his approval and so receives
the imprimatur of his own eternal being, is thereby made part of
the unshakable kingdom, like a bush that burns without being
consumed.

I cannot take my final picture from the Fourth Gospel, since the
"world" of John the Evangelist is from start to finish the world of
human response and responsibility. I take it therefore from the work
of the other John, from the climax of the Apocalypse; or rather,
from its double climax. For one of the pecularities of this re-
markable book is that its principal eschatological symbols (the
court scene, the wedding, and the battle) have a double fulfilment,
first within history before the millenium and then beyond history
in the new heaven and earth. At first reading we may receive the
impression that, while the millenium is the vindication of God's
purposes within history, the new heaven and earth are discon-
tinuous with the old ones which have been rolled up like a scroll.
But this is to take the imagery too pedantically. For we are told
that into the New Jerusalem shall be brought the wealth and
splendour of the nations, though nothing unclean may enter it
(21. 26-7). Not only are the gates of the city open on all sides to

receive the numberless company of its citizens. Everything of real worth in the old heaven and earth, including the achievements of man's inventive, artistic, and intellectual prowess, will find a place in the eternal order.

The only life after death that is either credible or desirable is a share in the eternity of God. But this must surely include a share in the joy with which God rejoices over his own creative works. And if man has been created not only to appreciate but to complete the work of God, he need not appear empty-handed when he enters into the joy of his Lord.

2

CAN CHRISTIANITY DO WITHOUT AN ESCHATOLOGY ?

WOLFHART PANNENBERG

In modern theology until very recently there was a strong tendency to minimize the importance of eschatological questions. Many theologians preferred and still prefer to concentrate on the possibilities and depth of present experience and on the urgencies of present action in contrast to the dubious future of a life after death, a final judgement for all men, and an end of the present world. This attitude did not emerge, however, without preparation. Even in the ancient Church, after the controversy about Montanism, eschatology was enshrined in, and limited to, the last chapter of history and of dogmatics. This is especially true of the final systematization of that dogmatic tradition which was achieved for the Protestant side in the "orthodox" dogmatics of the seventeenth century. Its eschatology had little to do with its understanding of Christ and the Church and of the present experience of the Christian. Divine providence, incarnation and atonement, the sacramental life of the Church, and the dialectic of Christian existence—all this was understood as independent of eschatology. Although eschatological salvation was considered to be the final goal and outcome of the divine action in Christ and of the mission of the Church, this outcome was expected as the future result of what, prior to it, happened in the past and in the present. Thus it became possible to concentrate on that past and present for its own sake and to dismiss the traditional eschatology, at least to the degree in which it seemed to be in conflict with the new understanding of nature as an unending process governed by unchanging laws.

Eighteenth-century criticism of the biblical writings favoured such an adaptation of Christianity to the spirit of the time. Thus Johann Salomo Semler, in his apologetics against the Wolffenbüttler Fragments edited by Lessing from 1774 onwards, tried to separate Jesus from the Jewish ideas which Reimarus, the author of those

fragments, had identified with Jesus' teaching. Semler dismissed such Jewish ideas, including the apocalyptic expectations, as foreign to Jesus' true mind. In using these eschatological ideas Jesus had only adapted himself to what Semler regarded as the limited comprehension of his Jewish contemporaries. Only in this way did Semler find it possible to defend the originality of Jesus and of the Christian religion. Accordingly, when he defended the resurrection of Jesus against Reimarus' criticism, he did so by spiritualizing the tradition and thus separating it from the allegedly crude Jewish conceptions.

This attitude towards the elements of Jewish apocalyptic in the New Testament has lasted until this day among New Testament scholars. The inclusion of the apocalyptic ideas concerning the future of man and the world in the category of "myth" by Bultmann and his school, alongside the three-storied universe and the belief in demons, indicates an unbroken continuity with Semler's prejudices.

In fact, however, neither Semler nor Lessing dispensed with eschatology altogether. They replaced the biblical conceptions by ideas corresponding to the two main aspects of it which may be called *individual* and *social* eschatology. Later on, both these aspects were systematically treated by Immanuel Kant. But while in the biblical tradition the individual eschatology of judgement and resurrection from the dead is closely connected with the social eschatology of the kingdom of God, these two aspects fell apart in the process of their reinterpretation in the eighteenth century. Individual eschatology was rephrased in terms of the immortality of the soul which had to face eternal life or judgement immediately after the death of the individual. Social eschatology was interpreted in terms of a perfect society which was conceived as the goal of the history of mankind. In this secular reinterpretation of the destiny of man its two aspects, social and individual, were no longer essentially related. If the individual is going to be eternalized immediately after his death, he has, apparently, no longer any essential relation to the destiny of society. And if society really achieves its human perfection in some future phase of its progressive development, what does such an attainment matter to the individuals of earlier generations who cannot enjoy the satisfaction of surviving to become part of it? In the biblical conception of the resurrection of individuals as an event which would come upon all of them at the end of time, the connection of the individual's future with the social destiny of the human race for a society of peace and justice in the kingdom of God was secured, since the general resurrection was considered the opening event of the kingdom. Here the destiny of the individual

is bound up with that of society, and of the human race in general, because the individuals of all historical periods have the chance to participate in the final perfection of the society of mankind, provided that they pass the divine judgement. The secularized eschatology could no longer do justice to the unity of human destiny, since it could not allow for a participation of individuals of past ages in a future society, if this perfect society was to be established in the course of history without any radical change of the natural structures of this world. The failure of secular eschatology in this respect seems rather to suggest that a *common* future of the individual beyond death and some "supernatural" character of the perfect society must be the pre-conditions of that common destiny. It is interesting that Lessing still felt the need that all individuals should have a share in the goal of human history: he went as far as playing with the idea of metempsychosis, which indeed would provide a possibility for individual souls to participate in the social life of a distant period of human history without changing the ordinary character of the natural conditions of that period in the way biblical eschatology does. With the idea of metempsychosis, of course, Lessing had to pay the price of surrendering the identity of human individuals with their particular bodily existence. At this point the integrity of the individual was lost again in Lessing's attempt to construct an image of the fulfilment of human destiny.

In the nineteenth century not only the secularization, but the abrogation, of eschatology was put on the agenda. The starting-point for this was Hegel's insistence that the realization of human nature cannot be adequately dealt with as a mere postulate, as was the case in Kant and Fichte. The human phenomenon as *human* phenomenon already presupposes the truth of humanity, the reconciliation between the common nature and destiny of man and his individual existence. Historically, this reconciliation was achieved for Hegel in Christ, because in Christ God and man were united and the destiny of man was thus completed—and this in the form of individual existence. The presence of the Absolute in Christ and through his spirit rendered any eschatologies superfluous because everything was already there. Admittedly, Hegel did not himself urge the critical consequences for eschatology of his doctrine of reconciliation. But eschatological statements are conspicuously rare in (indeed, almost absent from) his philosophy of religion. The idea of immortality was bound up with present participation in God. Here, if anywhere, we have a type of Christianity which apparently can do without an eschatology. Therefore, some of Hegel's followers could openly dismiss the eschatological tradition, especially the ideas of individual future beyond death, as an expres-

sion of an immoderate egotism on the part of the individual. They did not simply proclaim what Hegel had in mind, however, because they played down the importance of the individual over against the power and perfection of the human race, while Hegel himself considered the individual an essential element of the truth of the idea, even though the participation of the individual in that absolute truth has to take place, according to his view, in this present life. Nevertheless, the left-wing followers of Hegel, especially D. F. Strauss and L. Feuerbach who deeply influenced Karl Marx, remained true to Hegel in their conviction of the presence of the Absolute.

These left-wing Hegelians, of course, were by no means typical examples of Christian thought, since they shifted the presence of God in humanity through Jesus Christ into the divine glory of mankind as such. And yet the underlying conviction of the presence of the Absolute on the basis (at least on the historical basis) of the incarnation, represents much more than just the speculative ideas of a few philosophers. Hegel shared this conception with the main stream of Christian tradition. In the context of modern thought, he analysed and reflected the logical structure and the relevance of the principle of a final and insurpassable reconciliation more rigorously than many Christian theologians did before him. It is true that he isolated the idea of reconciliation and turned it into the only centre of Christianity; but there was a tendency in the Christian tradition to do so long before Hegel. This indicates the particular value of the rigorous examination and evaluation which the idea of reconciliation received in Hegel's thought. It presents an example of what underlies the outlook of many Christian theologies, although it was rarely developed with similar consistency. The idea of reconciliation on the basis of the unity of God with man offers possibly the most solid foundation for a Christianity without eschatology. The present theological positions which apparently can do without an eschatology share substructures with Hegel's idea of a reconciliation that has been already achieved, or the presence of the Absolute. I think not only of Karl Barth's idea of Jesus Christ, the incarnate God, as the archetype of man, but also of the various positions which assert that the experience of faith as forgiveness of sin is the centre of Christianity, or—last but not least—the current conception that love is the only reality of God present among men. All these positions rely on the assumption that in Jesus Christ the definite reconciliation of God and man was established, so that the presence of God in love or forgiveness is not only a momentary event, but a constant and fundamental factor in human life.

This entire approach was undercut when people began to wonder whether man and his world are in fact reconciled to their destiny. It is not necessary here to mention all the names in philosophy and modern writing of those who to the contrary insisted that man is alienated from his true destiny. This experience of alienation contributed to another wave of atheism and gave rise, at the same time, to a new type of secular eschatology which fervently believes that man himself is on his way to realize his authentic existence—either a new and more human society, or the superman. The most influential form of this new type of secular eschatology is, of course, Marxism. It is an eschatology which starts by unmasking the ideological character of the belief in a reconciliation already accomplished in the human situation, and, going on from the exposure of actual alienation, demands change. The peculiar difficulty of this secular eschatology is, however, the expectation that man—who, it is recognized, is alienated from his true nature—will at the same time be able to overcome his alienation by himself. Is he really able to achieve true humanity when starting with his alienated personality? Is not the promise of true humanity rather something which enters from the outside into the alienated human situation, becoming effective there in spite of the continuing powers of alienation rather than mysteriously resulting from alienated humanity itself? And is not the very discovery of alienation conditioned by the presence of that promise of a fuller life in the consciousness of those to whom the present situation of man appears as alienated?

The idea of a reconciliation which supposedly was already accomplished has been challenged not only in secular discussion but also in theology. When Albrecht Ritschl in the late nineteenth century developed the view that Jesus founded the kingdom of God, a community governed by love which only needs to be extended in the course of Christian history, the New Testament scholar Johannes Weiss refuted him by showing that Jesus expected the kingdom of God in the future and as an action of God himself, man's part being only to receive it. Thus the final salvation, the presence of the ἔσχατον, was not yet at hand except by anticipation of that future. This means that the reconciliation of the world has been accomplished—but by anticipation. Suffering and evil and alienation among men have not yet been definitely overcome either in the society or in the individual life. The present signs of the powers of reconciliation, of love and peace and true happiness, can look precarious if not ambiguous, and certainly they are far from being characteristic of the actual course of events. There is an irreproachable truth in the argument that this world ought to look different if

there were a God or if the Messiah had come already. It takes the
eyes of faith to recognize in the faint traces of genuine love and
human concern the prefiguring of a new constitution of the entire
universe. Although it is by no means irrational to appeal to such
elements in our present experience in order to argue for the truth
of faith, the reconciling presence of the Absolute in our world is
far from being obvious and undeniable. It is just because the
presence of absolute truth and reconciliation in the present state of
the human world is somewhat less than evident, that trust in God
has to rely upon a past event, the history of Jesus, which encourages
a hope for a future which has not yet materialized. Thus the very
idea of reconciliation through Christ—which suggested to Hegel
and to his followers the presence of absolute truth and therefore
rendered superfluous the eschatological hope for the future—is
conditioned by eschatology. The presence of God's kingdom in
Christ, according to the message of Jesus, was only an anticipation
of God's future, and the reconciliation of the world in the cross of
Jesus represents the significance which his sufferings received in the
light of his resurrection. This in its turn was again but an anticipation of the future glory of God in all the universe. In historical as
well as in a systematic perspective the decisive reason why
Christianity cannot do without an eschatology is that the reconciliation of the world, the presence of God, and his kingdom through
Christ, have taken place only in the form of an anticipation of a
future which in its fullness has not yet materialized. Therefore, the
belief in the reconciliation of the world in Christ is itself based
upon eschatology while at the same time it corroborates the
Christian trust and hope in the future of God.

Christianity could leave the question of eschatology undecided,
if belief in reconciliation through Christ and in the presence of God
and his kingdom were independent of it. The most recent attempt to
suggest such a view was the exegetical theory, promoted by Dodd
in England and by Bultmann in Germany, that according to Jesus
the eschatological kingdom of God, which Jewish religion expected
for the future, occured through his own ministry. Now there can
be little doubt that Jesus indeed emphasized the presence of the
kingdom in his own ministry and that this belongs to the heart of
his message. But this provides no justification for playing down the
importance of the words which refer to the future kingdom. The
true problem is hardly that of what could be dismissed as traditional
and what regarded as irreducibly particular and authentic in Jesus'
message; the real task seems rather to be to discover how both
aspects can be related in an adequate understanding of Jesus'
message. And because the futurity of the kingdom was the general

perspective in Judaism, it seems more natural to start with it and then try to understand the presence of the kingdom as the qualification of the present situation by that future.

If this exegetical diagnosis comes close to being adequate, then eschatology is no longer a marginal problem of theology, which one could leave to the last chapter of dogmatics, but the basis upon which everything in Christian tradition is built. Seemingly this had been realized by theologians under the impact of the work of Weiss and Schweitzer, when Karl Barth in the early 1920s said that theology must be thoroughly eschatological. But he—and similarly Bultmann—thought of a non-temporal eschatology. Barth and Bultmann sufficiently emphasized that God is not an object in the world of human experience and that there is no evident reconciliation of human suffering and frustration; but this led them, not to the question of future fulfilment, but to their emphasis upon the authority of God and his word in contrast to man, and to the demand for faith in that authority in spite of all contrary evidence. The removal of the time element in eschatology resulted in an authoritarian supernaturalism which not only violated the exegetical evidence but also the modern spirit of rational autonomy which necessitated the transformation of "orthodox" dogmatics in the eighteenth century. On the other hand, this process of transformation led to a secularized reinterpretation of eschatology which—as has been mentioned already—ended not with the total abolition of the eschatological problem but with a reopening of the quest for a future fulfilment of human destiny in individual as well as in social life.

The renewed eschatological emphasis deriving from the incongruity between the actual human situation and the destiny of man has consequences not only for the idea of reconciliation, but also for the idea of God. In some sense atheism has a point in arguing that the world ought to be different if there were a God who cares for man and even for every individual. The question whether the power of God is manifesting itself is not to be evaded. The Christian answer to this can be that the kingdom of God has not yet been established. It is still a matter of the future. Therefore in some way the question of the reality of God himself cannot be settled in a definite form. The kingdom of God is God himself and a God without power would be a God without reality. Hence only the full manifestation of God's kingdom in the future—which at the same time will bring about the definite realization of human destiny and thus the final reconciliation of God with his creation—can finally decide about the reality of God. This consideration allows a more positive Christian evaluation of a situation which has been characterized by

3

the phrase that God is dead. In the final analysis the Christian faith cannot agree with this phrase, but, with respect to the present condition of the world and of mankind, the absence of God and of his power is an experience which can be overcome only by anticipation of a future manifestation of what is so conspicuously absent at present. Such an anticipation, of course, needs an adequate basis, but, even if there is sufficient evidence for it, it remains an anticipation. The inability of man to overcome his alienation by himself calls for a power that endows man with that freedom. But even if we experience this power now, this must never again make God a being, alongside other beings in the world, which we have at our disposal. God as an extant being is a contradiction in terms. It would either mean the exclusion of human freedom or it would make him an object of human subjectivity and thus deprive him of his divinity. Paradoxically, both these disastrous consequences are involved in the traditional doctrine of God. If there is sense in conceiving of God as the origin of freedom, that experience has itself the character of anticipation and is not a statement about a being within the objective world of present reality.

The modern discussion of the question of human destiny, and even some of the arguments underlying modern atheism, seem to converge with the exegetical evidence towards a renewal of an eschatological outlook in Christianity and especially in Christian theology. But in following that suggestion one has to stand up against serious difficulties which tend to discourage any attempt to reconstruct Christian theology on the basis of eschatology. After all, it was not by accident that modern Christian thought tried to disengage itself from the tradition of Christian eschatology. The difficulties which burden it become again and again arguments for a Christianity without eschatology.

The advantage of traditional Christian eschatology, outweighing all attempts at its secularization, was its ability to reconcile the destiny of the individual with that of society. At its basis there was a combination of the idea of a resurrection of the dead with that of a future kingdom of God. That combination, however, provided the peculiarly transcendent and supranatural tinge of Christian eschatology which makes it so difficult to reconcile it with the modern understanding of nature. Is it really essential for Christianity to expect an end of this natural world and its radical transformation as a condition of the fulfilment of the destiny of man?

Certainly, there is a fundamental relation between the particular eschatological ideas of resurrection, judgement, eternal life, and the kingdom of God and the expectation that the present world will come to and end and will be replaced by, or transformed into, a

reality of a different kind. This relation is fundamental because individual eschatology is bound up with the final destiny of all mankind, which will not occur before the end of historical time. This might not require the assumption of an end of the natural universe as well, although the idea of a resurrection of the dead seems to imply so fundamental a change in the conditions of reality that it becomes difficult to imagine how the natural universe could remain unaffected by it. Be this as it may, there is a more general problem involved. Just how we are to conceive the relation between the highly symbolical eschatological language and the end of the world, is not quite clear. It is not necessary to identify the traditional sequence of eschatological events—historical and cosmological crises, resurrection, judgement, glorification, kingdom of God—with a sequence of events at the end of the world's history. The connection could be different and more complicated. This is suggested by the important fact that the eschatological ideas do not refer only to the end of time but also to the present. Thus resurrection and judgement must not be understood as expected events in a distant future without substantial continuity with the present. If conceived in that way, they are burdened wih all sorts of unanswerable questions such as that of the continuity between my physical existence now and events in a distant future maybe millions of years ahead. In fact, the tradition assumed a direct relation between eschatological events and the present time. The content of these events is nothing else than the content of our present life, but related to God's eternity and to the total context of history. Thus the content of the eschatological events is in no way foreign to our present life, and yet it is our present life in a different perspective from that in which we experience it now. It is evident that the question of the relation of time to eternity has a great deal to do with that of the particular reality to be ascribed to the statements of eschatological hope. Perhaps what is expressed in the language of a sequence of events easily confused with an ordinary historical sequence, should be interpreted in terms of the presence in and to our experience of the whole of our life in the context of all history and in its evaluation by God. In this way, it would become an open question what might be the concrete relation of eschatology to the end of history. It might become more understandable, on the other hand, how eschatological reality can foreshadow itself in present experience. And thus it might become less easy to dismiss eschatology as absurd and unacceptable. Eschatological ideas can be explained as a rationally lucid projection of the conditions for a final realization of human destiny in the unity of individual existence and social interrelatedness. In this sense eschatology is intrinsically

rational, although it expresses that destiny in symbolical terms. Symbolism, again, is not necessarily mere fancy. In its own way it may relate to the reality of our ordinary experience. It embraces that reality in its totality of meaning and therefore in another form than, say, scientific language. Thus the symbolic language of eschatology does not refer to a completely different kind of reality from that which we experience, but it articulates the element of mystery in the one world and in the one life which is ours. And the need for such an articulation might be the final answer to the question whether Christianity could not do better without an eschatology.

3

THE CONCEPT OF
THE ETERNAL

I. T. RAMSEY

THE concept of the eternal has traditionally embraced two concepts, one relatively clear and the other very puzzling. What I hope to do in this paper is to distinguish these two concepts; then to indicate some of the problems which consequently arise; and finally to make some suggestions as to how these concepts can be constructively related.

At the start of a notable paper on the subject,[1] Professor W. C. Kneale reminds us that these two concepts of the eternal can be distinguished by using the words "eternal" and "sempiternal".

> In the *Oxford English Dictionary* the first meaning of the word "eternal" is explained by the phrase "without beginning or end, that has always existed and always will exist". Clearly the authors are right to put this entry first; for the Latin *aeternus* is a contraction from *aeviternus*, and this in turn is derived from *aevum*, which contains the same root as the English words "ever" and "aye". In Greek the corresponding adjectives αἰώνιος and ἀΐδιος are even more obviously connected with the notion of everlasting existence; for αἰώνιος is derived from αἰών which in turn is derived from ἀεί meaning "always", and ἀΐδιος seems to have been formed directly from the same adverb. Here then we have the original sense of the word "eternal" and probably also that which is still the most common.[2]

It will have been noticed that in his explication Professor Kneale makes no explicit mention of time, though I think this is implied throughout, for Professor Kneale seems to suggest that this notion is better expressed by the word "sempiternal", where "sempiternal" is "lasting for ever" in the sense of "being there always at every moment of time", where time is thought of as an infinite series of moments. In other words, something is eternal in this sense if there

[1] *Proceedings of the Aristotelian Society* (1960-61), pp. 87-108.
[2] Loc. cit., p. 87.

is no moment when it is not there. So far as I am aware, we owe the word "sempiternal" in recent philosophical discussion to A. E. Hallett who introduced it into his exposition of Spinoza in the book *Aeternitas*, and where he found it necessary to distinguish between this notion of everlastingness in time—the actual duration characterizing *natura naturata*—and the kind of eternity about which Spinoza spoke, whether it be the real duration (*durée réele*) of the *conatus*, or the much more difficult sense in which there is in his view something eternal about each of us. Spinoza aside, this concept of sempiternity has been further refined by Professor C. D. Broad who, in his *Examination of McTaggart's Philosophy*,[3] has distinguished between what he calls an absolute sempiternity which is infinite at each end—past and future—and sempiternity which is infinite at one end only, which he distinguishes as retrospective sempiternity (which I suppose some physicists would attribute to the world) and prospective sempiternity (which some Christians have attributed to human souls).

Here is the relatively clear concept which is embraced within the concept of the eternal, and it is the concept of the eternal for which, by and large, empirically minded philosophers of religion such as F. R. Tennant and John Laird have settled. At the same time, let us realize what a sophisticated concept this is. For let us ask ourselves: From where do we get this notion of a doubly infinite series of moments? The answer is that it goes back to the "present" which we all experience as such, the present which the psychologists call in a most misleading way the "specious present", a present which always has some finite duration, which is characterized by a time flow whereby we distinguish earlier and later than, and in which there occurs a set of events. The notion of a "moment of time" is, then, a construction from the events given in such a specious present, and it is reached by choosing such events in the specious present as fall into a Chinese-box-like series whereby one event overlaps yet another event. Such a case, for example, would be when during an aircraft's passing overhead, a person starts and stops whistling, during which period a bell strikes, within which a watch ticks, and so on. A "moment of time" is then defined in terms of such a converging series of events. These moments of time are then ordered by means of that relation of temporal flow which (as I said) characterizes the specious present from which these moments of time have been abstracted. Here, very briefly and extremely crudely, is (as some readers will recognize) what Whitehead spoke of as the method of extensive abstraction. Whether it yields a sempiternity

[3] Vol. 2, Part 2.

bounded at one end, or doubly infinite, retrospective, prospective, or absolute in Broad's sense, must be for the facts to decide. But it is important that we should realize that this notion of "lasting for ever", if interpreted in terms of an infinite series of moments, is a highly sophisticated concept, though in principle not otherwise puzzling. Further, the notion of there being an upper bound to an infinite sequence might offer us some clue to the logic of such phrases as "the end (or beginning) of Time", the Last Day, and so on.

It is when we pass to the other concept that troubles begin to arise. Professor Kneale continues his exposition by contrasting with "sempiternal", "eternal" in a second sense—one (as he says) "which the authors of the *O.E.D.* call metaphysical and try to render by the phrase 'not conditioned by time' ".[4] The general problem which now arises is this: Can we think of the eternal, or eternity, in this second sense in any intelligible way which does not interpret it in terms of sempiternity or the sempiternal? Alternatively, and in particular, can we think of eternal life in an intelligible way which does not think of it as a life "lasting for ever"? Kneale himself in his paper spells out the problem in two ways:

1. He notes that St Thomas Aquinas in the *Summa Theologica* contrasts *eternity* with both *aevum* and time.

> But [says Kneale] in practice eternity and *aevum* are described only negatively, i.e., by removal of some of the features of time, and we are therefore left with no clear understanding of the system.[5]

Professor Kneale concludes summarily that

> at the best it seems that eternity is a highly refined version of time, and yet this must be wrong, since, as Augustine insisted very strongly, eternity is really timelessness.[6]

2. The second difficulty for Kneale arises around the phrase "eternal life".

> For [he says] I can attach no meaning to the word "life" unless I am allowed to suppose that what has life acts. No doubt the word "acts" may itself be taken in a wide sense. Perhaps it is not essential to the notion of life that a living being should produce changes in the physical world. But life must at least involve some incidents in time, and if, like Boethius, we suppose the life in question to be intelligent, then it must involve also awareness of the passage of time. To act purposefully is to act with thought of what will come about after the beginning of the action.[7]

4 Loc. cit., p. 87.
5 Loc. cit., p. 100.
6 Ibid.
7 Loc. cit., p. 99.

So, he would conclude, "timelessness" and "life" are two incompatible notions. In short, on this view, the more we try to remove the temporal reference from the concept of the eternal, the more we distinguish it from sempiternity, the more would we seem to drain the phrase "eternal life" of meaning.

What can we do then to clarify the concept of the eternal and to relate it to sempiternity? Let us now look at some of the traditional answers to this problem—for which I am much indebted to Professor Kneale's paper—and then at the end I hope to make some suggestions of my own.

First let us consider Parmenides with whom, says Professor Kneale, is the first appearance of the concept of eternity and it is introduced in contrast to what is changing. Broadly speaking, Parmenides was shocked by contemporary doctrines of universal flux and change which he supposed necessarily hostile to religion whose concern was with what abides. In contrast to such doctrines of universal flux, he claimed that there was a One which "is now all at once, a single whole", a One which, as Professor Kneale says, "cannot be described properly in language which employs tenses".[8] In other words, such a One, such a whole, while it contains time, cannot itself be said to be in time. Here is supposed to be a "mode of existence which allows"—presumably in regard to itself though not in regard to what it contains—"no distinction between past, present, and future".[9] It would appear that Parmenides commonly talked of this One "as though it were a great lump of stuff";[10] and it is interesting to recall that if, as is plausible, Parmenides accepted the religious teaching of Xenophanes, then this whole would be an everlasting god. But, leaving these detailed possibilities and developments aside, here, with Parmenides, we have the concept of the eternal developed in contrast to a doctrine of universal change, and its relation to time is modelled in terms of a Whole and its parts, in that we speak of a Whole which "contains" time. It might seem that historically this has been the favourite solution, if solution it can be called at all. We may say that this was the view broadly taken by Hegel and Bradley, by Spinoza, and by McTaggart.

For another solution we naturally pass to Plato where the Forms or Ideas are eternal, and we are reminded of the famous passage in the *Timaeus*:

> When the father and creator beheld the creature which he had made moving and living, the created image of the eternal gods, he rejoiced and in his joy determine to make the copy still more like the

8 Loc. cit., p. 88.
9 Loc. cit., p. 92.
10 Loc. cit., p. 89.

original. And as this was an eternal living being, he sought to make the universe eternal, so far as might be. Now the nature of the original living being is eternal, but to bestow this attribute in its fullness on a creature was impossible. He resolved therefore to make a moving image of eternity, and when he set the heaven in order, he made an everlasting image which moves according to number while eternity itself rests in unity. This is what we have called time. For there were no days and nights and months and years before the heaven was created, but when he constructed the heaven he devised them also. They all are parts of time, and "was" and "will be" are created species of time which we in our carelessness mistakingly apply to eternal being. For we say that it was, is, and will be; but in truth "is" applies to it, while "was" and "will be" are properly said of becoming in time.[11]

On this view, time is something which is related to eternity as a projection is related to that of which it is a projection. The sequence of moments of time points to some kind of centre. Time is related to eternity as a "moving image" is related to what it portrays, as the successive pictures on a cinema screen are related to what they survey from a succession of positions. It is perhaps worth noting that Plato did not deny the reality of time while glorifying the eternal. Further, it would seem that Plato grounded his concept of the eternal in some kind of experience which, at least in the earlier dialogues, he spoke of in terms of reminiscence. As Professor Kneale says,

> In his early works such as the *Meno* and the *Phaedo* he tried to explain the possibility of *a priori* knowledge by a doctrine of reminiscence which involves the hypothesis that before this life human souls lived among the timelessly existent Forms and contemplated them directly as in this life they see chairs and other things belonging to the realm of becoming.[12]

But the more sophisticated and detailed picture in the *Timaeus* is that by which the system of the Forms is regarded as a timeless model, perhaps something like a mathematical plan (to mention a suggestion to which I shall return later), a timeless model used by the demiurge, or craftsman, who made the temporal world.

Kneale rightly finds difficulties about this concept. He says:

> Yet . . . this . . . timeless model is said to be itself alive. Is this to be taken seriously? It is asserted in solemn fashion, and I think that it

---

[11] *Timaeus* 37E6—38A6, as quoted by Kneale, loc. cit., pp. 92-3. Kneale adds, as a footnote, the remark that "In the phrase 'everlasting image' I have deliberately introduced a new translation for αἰώνιος, since Plato seems to intend here no more than unending duration."

[12] Loc. cit., p. 99.

probably should be regarded as serious in view of the warning which Plato puts into the mouth of *Timaeus* at the beginning of the lecture : "In speaking of the copy and the original we may assume that words are akin to the matter which they describe. When they relate to the lasting and permanent they should be lasting and unalterable and, as far as their nature allows, irrefutable and invincible—nothing less. But when they express only the copy or likeness and not the eternal things themselves, they need only be likely and analogous. As being is to becoming, so is truth to belief."[13] Unlike medieval theologians, Plato seems to maintain here that discourse about the eternal is to be understood in the strict and primary sense of the words it employs, while discourse about the temporal is to be understood as analogical.[14]

Further, he has said earlier that Plato "probably came to realize that there is something absurd in the suggestion that a soul may pass part of its time in a timeless realm and then at a certain date enter the temporal realm".[15] Indeed, says Kneale, it is probably for this reason that Plato drops the doctrine of reminiscence in the later dialogues, and instead of glorifying the soul by treating it as something akin to the timeless forms, he there places it as the source of motion.

But suppose that we set these detailed difficulties aside and take much less of a pseudo-scientific view of Plato's metaphysics. Then we might say that, in his earlier philosophizing, Plato had in mind a strange situation that he called "reminiscence", where men became aware of their transcendence of the time series. Later in his philosophizing, he had in mind the somewhat less puzzling and certainly more familiar situation of human activity, something, however, still puzzling enough to have to be talked about in terms of a "soul" as the "source of motion", so that here, in this activity, men were again aware of their transcendence, and it was in terms of these transcendent situations that men talked of being aware of eternity.

We next pass to Augustine who incorporated a reference to the *Timaeus* passage in his *de Civitate Dei*, and again there seems to be implied a projection model, as well as the model of a whole and part, by which to relate eternity and time. God had an "eminence", the eminence of "ever present eternity", which was an eminence not only over the past. The Latin word is *celsitudine*, a moral eminence, a high advantage, something lofty or high, something which puts the temporal in perspective, and this "surpassed" all future times. It surpassed all future moments of time in so far as it

13 *Timaeus*, 29B.
14 Loc. cit., p. 100.
15 Loc. cit., p. 99.

outstripped, or abounded beyond, them while at the same time including them. So it was that God's years stand all at once: *omnes simul stant*. To know what God is like we must so talk of his years that they point again to a Whole—"that which stands all at once", or, to change the model, they point to that of which they are a projection. We might think indeed—though this is a point to which I shall return later—that this Whole "stood at once" like a whole person "stands at once" despite his changing expression in temporal terms.

We now pass to Boethius who very much continues Augustine's line of thought. For Boethius, "eternity" reveals the nature and knowledge of God and in this way "God" and "eternity" are logical kinsmen. Our moving makes unending time, he thought, whereas God's standing now makes eternity. Presumably Boethius did not distinguish between *human movement* which (as I showed by reference to A. N. Whitehead) makes unending time, and *our own activity* in which we can realize ourselves as transcendent, a whole which includes our temporal expression. However, to go back to Boethius' own words: "There is nothing established in time", he says, "which can establish the whole extent of its life without distinction. It does not grasp tomorrow, and it has already lost yesterday."[16] Though the life of something be endless, "it does not grasp and embrace the extent of it all at once (*totum simul*), but has some parts still to come".[17] Though the world is, says Boethius, everlasting, eternity is experienced by God as a *totum simul*, what I think we can best think of in terms of an extended "specious present". But to this model of a specious present, the projection model is added:

> Thus if you reflect on the immediate confrontation by which God discerns all things, you will judge that it is not foreknowledge of something as future, but rather knowledge of a never failing present. For which reason it is called not previdence but providence, because it is set far above the lowly details of the world and sees all things as though in a prospect from the highest summit. . . . Those future events which proceed from free will God sees as present. In relation therefore to God's sight of them and under the condition of divine knowledge they are necessary; but considered in themselves they lose nothing of the absolute liberty of their own nature.[18]

Boethius leads naturally to St Thomas who can be seen in effect as linking together both Boethius and Parmenides. St Thomas is well aware of what I have called two concepts of the eternal. As we have

---

[16] *de Consolatione Philosophiae*, v, 6; quoted by Kneale, loc. cit., p. 95.
[17] Loc. cit., p. 96.
[18] *de Consolatione Philosophiae*, v, 6; quoted by Kneale, loc. cit., p. 96.

seen, for St Thomas "the eternal has neither beginning nor end" and "eternity contains no succession, being all at once (*tota simul existens*)".[19] "Contains no succession" is rather "lacks succession". The Latin is *successione caret*, wanting, lacking, destitute of, succession. Though it is true that St Thomas never thinks of knowing eternity except through time, it might be argued that for him eternity is reached by thinking away time rather than by fulfilling it.

To this historical outline should be added another brief section in order to mention a very common interpretation of the eternal in terms of the timelessness of certain truths, especially mathematical truths. I mentioned this in my remarks about Plato. The main difficulty here, I think, is that on the face of it, even if there is a sense in which mathematical truths and all truths are "timeless", it does not seem to be a sense likely to be very helpful in relation to life, whether of man or God.

At the same time, I think the example could have wider significance on one or other of two possible interpretations. First, suppose we thought these timeless truths were reached by surveying a series of empirical generalizations. This parallel might then suggest that sempiternity provides somehow a route by which we understand what is meant by the eternal. On such a view the "timelessness" of the mathematical truth would break in on us at some stage of the empirical survey and so likewise would eternity. On the second interpretation, it might be claimed that these timeless truths gave us a true insight into any universe and so had a certain degree of empirical independence of the present universe, though they arose in it and with a relation to it. This might give us some understanding of how eternity could be other than the temporal, while in some way being related to it.

But now let me draw this series of examples together in making some suggestions of my own. It would seem as if talk of the eternal has always arisen as a particular way of talking about the sempiternal. According to Parmenides, who uses a whole–part model, the eternal can be thought of as a unity or whole of which sempiternity is a part. Another model for relating the eternal and the sempiternal has been to regard the eternal as a standpoint, a point of projection, of which the sempiternal is a moving image. This of course was a Platonic model. Another closely related model, found in Augustine, was that of the eminence from which sempiternity was a panorama, and this is closely related to the idea of the eternal (Boethius) as grasping and holding together within a kind of specious present

---

[19] *Summa Theologica*, Pars. I Quaestio x, Art. I; quoted by Kneale, loc. cit., p. 96.

what is serialized successively in sempiternity. For Augustine, the eternal is also that which excels, outstrips, or abounds and goes beyond sempiternity. For St Thomas the eternal is given as that which is deprived of, or freed from, succession, a view by which the eternal is not a highly refined version of time while being still in some sense temporal, but is a refined version in the sense that the eternal arises by thinking away time. Another model by which to relate eternity to time is that of the relation of mathematical Truth to a set of particular empirical generalizations.

My overall suggestion which generalizes from these models is that, to understand the eternal, we take time, and things in time, as we know them, accept the sempiternal for what it is, and then see eternity, and assertions about the eternal, as grounded in what I have called cosmic disclosures, which are reached in a variety of ways specifiable by the various sempiternal models. Let me show how this approach can absorb all I have said previously about traditional accounts of the eternal.

One route to a cosmic disclosure would be to survey a temporal series, conceived of as a succession of moments or instants, alongside a model of part and whole acting as catalyst, until there broke in on us a disclosure which was temporal and more. When this had occurred, we would refer to what had been disclosed as something which exceeded, outstripped, abounded beyond the sempiternity of the route by which it had been reached, this discourse being licensed by the particular model used in the disclosure; what had been disclosed would be beyond the succession of the terms which constituted the route for reaching it. We would point to the end product in terms of a metaphysical word such as "unity" or "whole".

Again I would suggest that if we are to speak of time being a "moving image" or panorama of the eternal, we must associate with time conceived of as a succession of instants models like standpoint, point of projection, eminence, along with their associated panoramas, in the hope that around the temporal panorama there will be evoked a disclosure of the eternal which is temporal and more.

In the case of the *nunc stans* or *totum simul* of Augustine and Boethius, it may be recalled that John Laird once suggested that when in certain cases we talk of the "now" it might be because our experience at that time "had or seemed to have the vividness and freshness of the present".[20] Such a suggestion, by incorporating words such as "vividness" and "freshness", implies that the word "now" can be so used as to be grounded in a disclosure, which occurs as we come to ourselves, and recognize "vividly" and

---

[20] *Theism and Cosmology* (Allen and Unwin 1940), p. 158.

"freshly" our existential status, on a particular occasion. We might then construe the *nunc stans*, the *totum simul*, the "absolute now" as a qualified model, in the sense that these reflections on the specious present, in which we first grounded the word "now", could then be broadened without limit until something "absolute", all-inclusive, disclosed itself to us.

I suggested that the technique of St Thomas was, for example, to take time—sempiternity—with its earlier and later, with its "innovation and aging", and then constantly to extend the sempiternity until there was a disclosure of what fulfilled the series. We may say that in effect St Thomas was appealing here to the model of a succession of terms, as a good clue to the sum of an infinite series, just as alternatively we might appeal to the notion of an irrational number given by a Dedekind section. In this sense sempiternity can by itself and without further models disclose a transcendent whole, as a sequence may disclose something of another logical order.

With the model of mathematical truth, where a survey of particular assertions might lead us to the intuition of the mathematical generalization, this would again be a catalyst to point us from sempiternity to that disclosure situation in which the concept of the eternal is grounded.

So far I have been concerned to talk of how we reach the situation which in the last resort justifies any talk about the eternal, and I think it is clear that with my terminology the eternal is a kind of end-point word for which we have models integrated with, and structured in terms of, sempiternity. On this view, we must not think we can talk about the eternal entirely independently of our talk about time. We can only talk of eternity through and in relation to time. We only understand how to talk about eternity by using temporal models structured in sempiternity. To talk about "eternal x", where x equals "life", "punishment", "love", and so on, is, I would say, so to talk about x in the context of sempiternity as to evoke a disclosure in which the concept of the eternal is grounded, when we then have on hand a word or phrase—x—which is licensed for discourse about the eternal.

By way of elucidating this standpoint, let me recall some sentences from an article by M. E. Ravicz in the *Thomist* for October 1959 on "Augustine and Time". Dr Ravicz remarks that for Augustine "love gives psychological time a *vertical* dimension", but he adds "eternity is 'horizontally' in the future". I would interpret this latter remark to mean that, to approach an understanding of eternity, we might survey a series of moments, which provides a temporal setting, for example, for friendship, and develop it into the future "horizontally". In other words, we experience eternity only by a disclosure

which "breaks in" on us, for example, as we survey friendship "horizontally"—I deliberately use that word "friendship" since we are concerned with a sempiternal survey. He next remarks "that we are compelled to realize and experience this eternity in a 'vertical' now". The disclosure character of eternity gives, it seems to me, the point of the word "vertical"—implying that something "breaks in" on us as we survey the horizontal series of terms. Dr Ravicz adds that "the dimension which can unite the two realms of time and eternity is love". What I would then say is that we may then take love as an end-point word when friendship has been contextualized in a temporal series to evoke a cosmic disclosure. Love is then a word which straddles across and holds together time and eternity. Not for nothing do people speak of love as a "timeless friendship", and we may recall C. A. Coulson's well-known example in *Christianity in an Age of Science* :

> It has been my privilege, as it must have been yours also, to know one or two old couples, Darby and Joan, who have lived together, and grown together, over many years of happy married life. When I have met them, it has sometimes seemed as if, sitting on either side of the fireplace, they had grown so much alike that in some sense they merged into one another. . . . Such people are a sign to me that when the things that bind two characters together are sufficiently important, these characters influence each other so deeply that their personalities merge into one. You can scarcely tell where one begins and the other ends. The knowledge, the experience, the hopes of one become the property of the other also. . . . In fact, these two are one : and the life of the one is the life of the other, and his fulfilment too. We outsiders know this for we have glimpsed it in odd revealing moments.[21]

It is such a "revealing moment" which fulfils time in eternity.

Plainly the concept of God will also be a concept which straddles the eternal and the temporal. When people say that "for God *futura iam facta sunt*", we must certainly not give this phrase the obvious and quite impossible logical structure which its verbal form at first sight suggests. But when we ground the word "God" in a cosmic disclosure, we are aware of a *factum* indeed, disclosure given, and it is a *factum* which includes what *futura* can increasingly and adequately talk about. Just as through temporal change we become aware of what abides, so the reliability of God is expressed through his sempiternity. Hence, as A. N. Whitehead pointed out, the popularity of the hymn "Abide with me", which provides a sempi-

---

[21] C. A. Coulson, *Christianity in an Age of Science* (University of Durham Riddell Memorial Lectures) (O.U.P. 1953), p. 52.

ternal survey of change and decay, at some point of which God may disclose himself as that which abides. We may recall Professor Kneale's remarks on page 89 of his paper :

> Men may be unconcerned about their own mortality, but they are not in general happy unless they can fix their minds on something permanent. In the earlier part of their history the Jews appear to have thought little or nothing about life after death but a great deal about the supreme power of God, and they liked to think that his Hebrew name meant "I am" or "I shall be".[22] Almost certainly it would be a mistake to suppose that they read into this word all that Parmenides tried later to convey by ἔστι, since they were not metaphysically minded and their language did not possess the Indo-European system of tenses, but I think they took it as an expression of the dependability of God.

Indeed they did.

My suggestion, then, is that talk of eternity or the eternal is a way of pointing, normally by various models, through sempiternity to what is more than the temporal. "The eternal" relates to what is disclosed to us as temporally transcendent, to what breaks in on us to complete, fulfil, and bound a doubly infinite temporal series. The eternal refers to that which breaks in on us in what I have called a "cosmic disclosure", a situation I think which has plain affinities with Platonic reminiscence disclosing the forms, or the awareness of motion disclosing the soul. So eternal life talks about life in such a way as to disclose a transcendent dimension to our present human existence.

Many will be nervous of, if not scandalized by, the idea of a situation which is partly spatio-temporal and partly "more". But let us realize that the "more" is not on logical all fours with the spatio-temporal. To the "eternal" we can only point; it breaks in on us rather than confronts us. In this way the eternal is given in a situation whose subjective element is a self-disclosure, and we may well come to see in this way the meaning of the phrase "timeless self". For when we survey ourselves in time, when we enumerate in David Hume's phrase a succession of distinct perceptions, then there may break in on us a disclosure which embraces, outstrips, abounds beyond, what in principle is an infinite time series. What is disclosed subjectively, ourselves, our subjectivity is something which has an eternal dimension and in that sense we are immortal, with an immortality expressible in terms of sempiternity.

Are the two notions of timelessness and life then incompatible? I would say not. If "life" can already refer to that which surpasses,

---

22 Exod. 3. 14.

abounds beyond, the sempiternal and is given in self-disclosure, then there is already a sense in which the phrase "eternal life" can have a legitimate use for us. Life is precisely that which, given in self-disclosure, can be talked of as eternal as much as it can be talked of as temporal. That this is odd can be readily granted. But, all that follows is that life is rather odder than what we otherwise have expected it to be.

But of course what we must guard ourselves against is the error of supposing that the "Whole" is reliably construed as some particular existent in a spatio-temporal universe. This is the general case of the particular mistake of supposing God to be one being among others. What Parmenides and Augustine and St Thomas spoke of as the "Whole" stands for what we are aware of when the sempiternal story, providing a setting for the model of whole and part, has its fulfilment. It stands for what breaks in on us, what is disclosed to us through such a temporal review. It is quite plain in the history of the subject that the eternal has been talked about in highly misleading ways, as when Parmenides would have regarded it as a great lump of stuff, or when it has been talked about more sophisticatedly as a "realm", leaving that word unqualified. It has also been wrongly talked about when it was pictured as the environment for a Platonic soul, which might drop in for a temporal break from its timeless existence.

Certainly, the eternal does not talk of a realm, as it might be supposed to do by counterpart contrast with the temporal. Nor does it talk of a quality, so that "eternal" life would be comparable in logic to a "quiet" or a "busy" life. Talk of the "eternal", for example eternal x, is appropriate only when talk about something, x has been set in a temporal framework structured in sempiternity as I have expressed it, and so developed that it has led to that which includes and transcends x, fulfils it in a disclosure. But now I would remark, linking together points I have made both earlier and more recently in this paper, that for me the paradigm for a disclosure of the eternal is self-disclosure, and so it is not surprising that it is to highly personal words that people have turned when they wanted discourse about the eternal. Witness: Augustine and love. Personal immortality—as life in sempiternity—must always be construed as a means of talking of our eternity.

A last word on the well-known verse in St John's Gospel,[23] in the controversy with the Jews: "Jesus said unto them, 'Verily, verily, I say unto you, Before Abraham was, I am'." In other words, "before Abraham was born", that is, before Abraham came into being,

[23] 8. 58.

before he had an existence in the time series initiated by birth, "I am". Here is the "I am" of an absolute existent who includes and fulfils all temporal succession. It is *not* a case of antecedent existence in time. It is not "before Abraham came into being, I was". The point is well made by Cyril of Alexandria :

> He therefore is not rivalling Abraham's time, nor does he affirm that he is . . . precedent to his time, but since he is above all time, and overpasseth the number [numbering] of every age, he says he is before Abraham.[24]

In other words, to speak of Jesus as eternal is, first, to claim that when we speak, in terms of retrospective sempiternity, about anything whatever in the past, we must say that when it came into being Jesus was already existing (nor do I think that this necessarily conflicts with Cyril's point) and secondly that, when we carry out this exercise relating Jesus not only to all heroes of faith, but to all creatures and all created things, the eternity, the pre-existence, of Jesus is something disclosed to us.

I have tried, then, to suggest a way of combining the two concepts of the eternal and the sempiternal, which are embraced by the concept of the eternal as it is in general use. I have also tried to show the implications for specimen discourse about eternal life and love, and the interpretation I would offer of the pre-existence and eternity of Christ. My broad conclusion is that anything in time (life, or a moral quality, a condition, or a thing) can in principle be a model which, in the setting of sempiternity, can lead to what is thereby an all-inclusive cosmic disclosure. Such a disclosure, which transcends and fulfils the model and its sempiterinity, will be a disclosure of what is eternal. This is to discover an "eternity" which can then be talked about in discourse licensed by the model, discourse structured in a temporal order. The concept of the eternal, the word "eternal", when used by itself, points to this permanent possibility of fulfilling the temporal. That is why, in my terms, "eternal" can work as a qualifier, related to sempiternity, not so much to be regarded as a model but as a presupposition of all models. Sempiternity is thus the setting which enables all models to be developed in the direction of that disclosure in which talk of the eternal is grounded, and in which eternity and sempiternity find their mutual placing and reconciliation.

---

[24] Quoted *The Fourth Gospel*, E. Hoskyns and F. N. Davey (Faber and Faber 1940), vol. II, p. 401 (Cyril of Alexandria, *In Ioannis Evangelium*, Lib. XII, *passim*).

4

THE MARXIST HOPE

JAMES KLUGMANN

WHAT I shall try to do here is to attempt to interpret what "hope" means, not so much in terms of philosophy, but to millions of men and women, *motivated*, moved, by Marxism, all over the world. For Marxists "hope" is a very meaningful word indeed. When, as a young student in the early 1930s, I first came towards Marxism, many, at Cambridge where I studied, just accepted things as they were; amongst others, perhaps the most thinking, there was an atmosphere of introspection and pessimism.

Suddenly, becoming a Communist, joining the Communist Party, I found myself as it were in a new world. The Hunger Marchers, unemployed workers tramping down from the North, came through Cambridge. They came from the depth of the so-called "depressed areas", but, instead of depression and despair, they seemed to be full of confidence, hope, and the strength derived from it. I made my first contact with working class revolutionaries. They were part of a small minority, yet they seemed to me very strong in their confidence.

I began to work in the international student movement against war and fascism. In the Balkans where the radical student movement was mostly illegal and where capture often meant torture, amidst the incredible poverty of India, or during the anti-Japanese war in China, or meeting the youth from the underground resistance of Nazi Germany, that is, amidst the most difficult and desperate circumstances, when many were indeed despairing, I met Marxists, young and old, again and again, strong and confident in hope. This was no empty word, no subtle scholasticism. Hope burned in them like a fire.

My thoughts go to the third volume of Jean-Paul Sartre's wonderful trilogy *Iron in the Soul*. The scene is amongst the captured French soldiers after the Nazi armies had swept over the country. Schneider

reproaches the communist Brunet. He finds it hard to understand him, to understand communists:

> "When I asked what you were hoping, I was perfectly right," said Schneider gloomily, "_You live on, hope_,"[1]

What, in the most general terms, is this Marxist hope, which seems to deepen life even on the point of death? I think it is understood that history is not a meaningless succession of accidents; that great revolutionary changes are necessary in the world; that a better future can be won for men, that man himself can change, can improve; that this change, this future is possible though not inevitable; that, in the last analysis, it depends on the conscious efforts of men.

Perhaps the essence of this Marxist hope, or should I say this hope of Marxists, for it is not only theirs, is that it is not just a vision of what society and man can be, _but the acceptance of the responsibility to make this come about_. It is active not passive, revolutionary not resigned. The hope leads to responsibility and action, thence back again to hope. Hope, then, for a Marxist, in its best sense (for the word is used colloquially too) lies not in a kiss of comfort, not in an escape from pain, not in a plea for mercy nor for help, but in a personal and collective contribution to social change, change of the world and, in the process, of man.

"Men Make Their On History"

A common misunderstanding of Marxism is that Marxists believe that in history all is _determined_. Marxists are supposed to deduce all things—past, present and future; social orders, science and art, God and man—from iron, unavoidable, uninfluenceable economic laws. For Marxists, it is said, all is fixed in advance. Where then is the place of men? And where, they could well add, is the place of hope?

It would be wrong to turn these brief remarks into an exposition of historical materialism, of the Marxist theory of social development. This is a complex approach, the product of long study, reflection, and discussion which still continues. Some of you will be familiar with it and of others who are not, I must beg permission to make assumptions. For us past history is not a series of accidents, a meaningless succession of events. In our view we can discern certain general laws of social development, and these, understood, can be taken into account and can help us to see the general shape of the possible future and to contribute consciously towards it, if you like to "speed it up". But these are not laws of the type of the natural

---

[1] Jean-Paul Sartre, _Iron in the Soul_ (Hamish Hamilton 1963 reprint), p. 338.

sciences. They are laws of tendency, and depend for their fulfilment on the action of men and women.

Marx and Engels took as their fundamental starting-point men and women in society fulfilling their most essential functions, securing food, clothing, shelter, and, in so doing, developing endlessly, and ever more speedily, the forces of production—their instruments and tools, their scientific and technological knowledge, their own skills. They came to see that, in the course of their social existence and social production, men entered into different relations of production, which corresponded to the given level of the forces of production. Their conception of production relations embraced the way in which men and women got their livelihood, the different social classes to which they belonged, with the essential issue of who owned and who did not own the means of production. Each form of social organization, each social formation, for a time corresponded to and encouraged the development of the productive forces, but at a certain stage became an obstacle for their further development. In Marx's famous words:

> In the social production of their life, men enter into definite relations that are indispensable and independent of their will, relations of production that correspond to a definite stage of development of their material productive forces. . . . At a certain stage of their develop-ment the material productive forces of society come into conflict with the existing relations of production—what is but a legal expression for the same thing—with the property relations within which they have been at work hitherto. From forms of development of the pro-ductive forces these relations turn into their fetters. Then begins an epoch of social revolution[2]

A new form of social organization became necessary, but it would not come by itself. New and rising social classes would fight for fundamental social change which would be bitterly resisted by the old ruling class. There would be long and complex struggle for revolutionary change. Thus Marx and Engels came to see, as it were, a pattern in history. In the infinitely complex intermingling of persons and events could be discerned beneath the surface an uneven process of development, not exactly the same in all parts of the world (they discussed for instance the character of the Asiatic mode of production as a stage of society in certain areas), but—roughly and very over-simplified—a succession of social formations from early classless tribal society (primitive communism) to slavery (not in all areas), feudalism, and capitalism, and thence to socialism and communism. They came to see, more than 120 years ago, that

2 Karl Marx, *Preface to the Critique of Political Economy.* 1859.

capitalism itself, under which science and technique had made such tremendous advances, was now becoming an obstacle to further development. That is, it was preventing not *all* development of science but its *potential* development, and above all its development and use for the service of man.

The vast concentration of wealth and the sources of wealth in the hands of a few private concerns and private individuals could not and would not be used in the interests of mankind. On the contrary, the ever more social form of labour made both possible and necessary a change to the *social* ownership of the means of production, the replacement of capitalism by socialism. In the dramatic and prophetic words of the *Communist Manifesto*,

> Modern bourgeois society with its relations of production, of exchange and of property, a society that has conjured up such gigantic means of production and exchange, is like the sorcerer who is no longer able to control the powers of the nether world whom he has called up by his spells.[3]

How much more urgently true are these words now in these days of cybernation, giddy advance of technology, space travel, when we are on the brink of limitless sources of power, but when the same science that can free the world from sordid material care can blow it to pieces!

> The solution [wrote Engels] can only consist in the practical recognition of the social nature of the modern forces of production, and therefore in the harmonizing of the modes of production, appropriation and exchange with the social character of the means of production. And this can only come about by society openly and directly taking possession of the productive forces which have outgrown all control except that of society itself.[4]

Conscious Men and Women

I do not, I am sure, need to impress on Christian theologians the dangers of what Marxists (borrowing, I believe, from Christianity) call dogmatism.

The fact that Marxists thought it possible to distinguish a general pattern in history, and, indeed, a general pattern of the shape of things to come, was by some (and sometimes, alas, in the name of Marxism), vulgarized into a sort of simple determinism. "Socialism is inevitable," they said, "that is all you know or need to know." This was (and is) dangerous, for it omits a most essential part of Marxist thinking. For Marxists, as I understand it, socialism is necessary, yes. It is the type of social organization that corresponds

[3] Karl Marx and Frederick Engels, *The Communist Manifesto*. 1848.
[4] Frederick Engels, *Socialism, Utopian and Scientific*.

to the present level of human techniques. It can lay the basis for the highest economic advance, the greatest freedom, and the best cultural and moral development, in our present situation. In the capitalist world it is overdue and urgent. *But, it will not come by itself. It will have to be fought for.* And this will be a long complex struggle, taking many forms, and led by the working class. Socialism is possible and necessary, but the need for it has to be consciously understood, and it has to be consciously won and built—*by men.*

That men make their own history was something that Marx and Engels were constantly repeating. "Men are both the products and makers of circumstances", wrote Marx when he was still a young man, in those famous notes or jottings that he wrote when studying the German philosopher Feuerbach, and that have come to be known as the *Theses on Feuerbach*:

> Men are products of circustances and upbringing, and, therefore, changed men are the products of other circumstances and changed upbringing. . . .

But he continues:

> It must never be forgotten . . . that circumstances are changed precisely by men and that the educator himself must be educated.[5]

There is no such thing, wrote Marx and Engels in *The Holy Family*, as an abstract History with a capital H, rolling on, compelling puppet man to do its inexorable bidding:

> History does nothing, it "possesses no immense wealth", it "wages no battles". It is man, real living man, that does all that, that possesses and fights; "history" is not a person apart, using man as a means for its own particular aims; history is nothing but the activity of man pursuing his aims.[6]

History is not something that exists outside the men that make it. Nor, as Marx saw, did men and women make history independently of past history or the society in which they lived. They did not create it at their pleasure, out of historical context:

> Men make their own history, but they do not make it just as they please, they do not make it under circumstances chosen by themselves, but under circumstances directly encountered, given and transmitted from the past.[7]

It was Marx's view that in history, right up to the establishment of capitalism, men in their efforts to bring about social change could

---

5 Karl Marx, *Theses on Feuerbach* (this is the third Thesis).
6 Karl Marx and Frederich Engels, *The Holy Family*, chapter 6.
7 Karl Marx, *The Eighteenth Brumaire of Louis Bonaparte*, chapter 1.

not foresee the exact form of society which they would bring into being. The fact, for instance, that the capitalist class, progressive in the fight against feudalism, were themselves exploiters, obscured as it were their vision. Men fought for "liberty, equality and fraternity", and got—capitalism.

But in the present struggle for socialism, when the aim was to move towards a society without exploitation, when the leading class in the struggle had as its aim a fully classless society, when they would have come to understand the general laws of social development, the revolutionaries could become fully conscious not only of the society and world that they wished to oppose and to end, but the society and world that they wished to win and construct.

Men would at last, fully consciously, struggle for a new society. They would envisage the general shape of things to come, and then proceed to make that vision a reality. Working men and women, *understanding*, would in *struggle* emancipate the world and themselves:

> As soon as the lightning of thought has struck deep into the virgin soil of the people they will emancipate themselves and become men.[8]

Predicting the Future

The Marxist conception of hope is deeply linked with the Marxist view that, in general terms, men can *predict* the shape of the future.[9] Looking at the overall development of human society from the earliest times, Marxism sees it as the progressive posing and tackling of a series of problems that stem from the development of the productive forces. This is not seen as an *inevitable* process. Marx made clear in his *Pre-Capitalist Economic Formation* that adaptation has sometimes been unsuccessful and led to a dead end rather than to further progressive development. The overall history of human society is thus seen as a law-governed process, but not in the strict determinist sense that there are preordained laws that allow nothing to happen except that which *does* happen. And so we see in general terms how we can build a future in which the inner contradictions of capitalism will be ended, in which our productive relations will again correspond to the now vastly extended productive forces, and in which in changing society men can change (and improve) themselves.

[8] Karl Marx, *Introduction to the Critique of Hegel's Theory of Law.*

[9] For a detailed discussion of the Marxist view of prediction, I recommend *The Open Philosophy and the Open Society*, by Maurice Cornforth (Lawrence & Wishart 1968) from whom I have borrowed heavily in this section on prediction.

But this prediction is for Marxists conditional and not un-conditional. We do *not* say that nothing can stop the establishment of socialism. Just as the *Communist Manifesto* (in 1848) wrote of the possible "mutual ruin of the contending classes", so even more clearly we can see that the future envisaged could be prevented by a nuclear war that physically destroyed the world or the human life in it (or for that matter, however unlikely, by an invasion from space). Above all, as Marxists, we insist that the future can be made but men and women have to make it. When, as Marxists, we make predictions about the future, they are predictions about human actions and the results of human actions. The people making the predictions are themselves agencies in the processes through which the predictions will be realized. To predict something in this Marxist sense, something in which you are involved either indi-vidually or through whom you support or with whom you are associated, with whose interests you identify your own, is equiva-lent to a statement of intent. And so, when we confidently, *hopefully* (I have not, I hope, forgotten that our subject is *hope*) predict a world of socialism and communism, we take it for granted that we, and those like us, people of certain classes (working class and its allies, national liberation forces, etc.) throughout the world, will strain every effort to make this prediction come true.

I remember, in his connection, a very angry reader's letter to the *Daily Worker* (precursor of our daily paper *The Morning Star*)

> You Communists [it said] are a lot of b———s. First you predict that something is going to happen. And then you work like mad, and try and get others to work, to make your prediction come true; this I call cheating!

Not cheating! This is the very essence of Marxism, and, incidentally, of Marxist hope.

The Shape of Things to Come

May I attempt, in all too few words and in over-simplicity, to con-vey to you something of this vision of the future that unites Marxists all over the world, despite what are often deep differences on tactics and strategy? What is this vision that continuously moves them to actions, humble and heroic, and sometimes to endure a difficult death? What is this vision which fills them with so much *hope*? It is the vision of a world (not worked out in detail like some Fourierist fantastic phalanstery[10]) that they will have to build or help towards

---

[10] Fourier was the French Utopian Socialist of the early nineteenth century. His *phalanstères* were socialistic communities envisaged as forming the best reorganization of Society.

the building thereof, of which they are hopefully confident that if
not they, then their children or their children's children will see
emerging, and to which they in any case will contribute.

As Marxists, in broad outline, we see two stages of developing
socialism, a first and a later, a lower and a higher, the one gradually
arising out of the other. In our own parlance of today, we usually
speak of the first stage as socialism, and the higher stage as communism.[11] We see in the first stage, socialism, a great advance compared with the preceding capitalist or imperialist society, but yet
a complex transitional society that emerges in struggle (usually
prolonged and bitter though not necessarily violent), and inevitably
bears at first many of the marks of the defects of previous society
whether acute deficiencies of goods, or of the character of men and
women, who even as they struggle for a revolutionary change of
society will inevitably carry in their heads and minds something of
the old outlooks and attitude of competitive and oppressive
capitalism.

Moreover, the fact that socialism first emerges in one or a group
of countries with their former rulers resisting and surrounded by
a bitterly hostile capitalist world, is itself an obstacle to the most
rapid and desirable forms of development of socialism. Socialism
therefore in our eyes is both a magnificent step forward and a
society itself in movement and change with many problems, contradictions and, inevitably, errors and weaknesses. The old ideas of
nationalism and racialism, lust for property and power, will die
hard. It is not an end nor a paradise, but a path of advance.

What do we see as the main differences between socialism and
communism, the two stages of socialist society? It is hard to
explain this in a few sentences.[12] We see with socialist society a
large and steady advance of production in a planned way, but not
by any means the possibility as yet of meeting all the needs of the
whole of the people. But as under socialism, production advances,
we see the possibility of reaching what Marx called *an abundance*
of goods, that is, enough to meet all the normal needs of all the
people, the ending for all time of the sordid scarcities of food and
clothing and shelter that still, despite the fantastic advance of
science and technology, are the hallmark of the greater part of the

[11] Writing of this in his *Critique of the Gotha Programme*, Marx (in 1815)
spoke of the lower and higher stages of communism.

[12] I have tried to explain it simply but at greater length in *What Sort
of Revolution* (Panther paperback 1968), ed. Paul Oestreicher and James
Klugmann.

world still dominated by imperialism. And abundance is the economic basis of communism.

We see under socialism (and this can be studied in the existing socialist countries) that goods will be distributed *according to work.* As men and women put into society, so they will be entitled to take out, whilst society as a whole will care for the old, the young, and the sick. But as production moves in the direction of abundance, and as men's outlook becomes more social, we see in communist society the possibility of distribution *according to needs.* The watchword of socialism is "from each according to his capacity; to each according to his work"; of communism "from each according to his capacity; to each according to his needs".

As socialism passes into communism, we see step by step the ending of men's alienation from their work, their society, and themselves, and how, when machines have taken over the monotonous, repetitive, dull, and back-breaking processes of which so much work today consists, and when people no longer feel that they toil for the profit of others rather than for their fellows and themselves, so work as Marx and Engels foresaw can become a pleasure, indeed life's prime want. We see as socialism is built and passes into communism the possibility of ending social classes, all exploitation of one class by another, of ending, indeed, all the essential differences between farmer and worker, between manual and mental worker. Communism will see a citizenry skilled, of many trades; it will see higher education; it will see manual and mental worker, working for society and, at the same time, for themselves. It will see, and this will be a prolonged process, the full emancipation of women—political, economic, and ideological—a problem, which you will forgive me for saying, the Christian Church seems grossly to have neglected. As the attitude of men and women becomes step by step more social and less selfish, the State and with it all the instruments of force—armies, police forces, and security organizations—can wither away, and whilst administration persists and becomes in some senses more complex, the old style state organs can be relegated to the museums of human history, as can war.

As socialist society is first constructed there will at first, perforce, be strong remnants, even in the minds of those who make the revolution, of racialism, nationalism, and other aspects of the old outlook. Frontiers will not die in a day. Problems will exist at first amongst socialist countries, just as socialist lands will have their crimes and contradictions. But step by step, with the profit motive excluded, it is our opinion that we shall proceed towards a single world, a brotherhood of man, a united humanity.

We do not at all see a development towards a dull uniformity.

Indeed, in our opinion, it is the limitations imposed on society by imperialism, the condemnation of most of mankind to an almost animal (even vegetable) existence along with a commercialized profit-making culture for those that can afford it, that produces a standardized, hardly human, "product". Most men and women under imperialism (if the Third World, as it must be, is counted) hardly exercise more than a tiny fraction of the vast potentialities within them, indeed are hardly conscious that they possess them at all. Development from socialism to communism will permit men and women to exercise their many-sided talents, to become many-sided people, people with a purpose, for, in our opinion, it is only as part of society that individual man can fully express himself. There is all the difference in the world between individualism and individuality.

Even as I try to explain to you something of the vision of the society in our opinion men and women can build if they end capitalism and take the road of socialism and communism, I feel a certain misgiving. I am going too fast. Time is a tyrant to readers of papers. I am leaping decades in a second. I am not elaborating all the many—endless—problems, difficulties, mistakes. We do not at all think that building socialism and communism is either easy or inevitable. It is a prolonged complex process. It will involve ups and downs, victories and setbacks. It will not be without struggle, nor error, nor at times crime. Nor do we see even communism as an end to man's efforts and advances. The question is often asked: "What is the 'ultimate aim' of Marxists?" Our discussion posed the problem: Can there be a perfect society on earth? Marxists would answer no. We have no *ultimate* aim. We see the possibility of, and we work for, a world where all poverty and exploitation is ended, where war is a thing of the past, where there is no more antagonistic division of class or nation or of race, and where, as part of society, each man and woman can develop fully his or her many-sided and vastly varied talents and capacities. But to say this is not to postulate an *end*. We can see no end to the process of men struggling to improve the world and themselves, no end to problems and contradictions within society and within men and women. We see an eternal vista of new problems and new efforts to solve them. We can see no end to hope.

Marxists are not magicians and do not (or should I say should not?) claim to be. They cannot see beyond a certain point in the shape of the future. But the point that we think that we see is more than enough to inspire us to action, and the fact that, when that point is reached, there will be new visions of new futures ahead of us, and that new men and women will have new hopes and seek to

realize them, satisfies us, I think, more than any fantasy of paradise achieved, or a final end.

We see no *ultimate* end. But we know what we *can* get rid of, and speedily—the sordid misery of hunger, widespread disease, insecurity that bedevils life, war and the haunting fear of it, the exploitation of man by man, racial and national hatred, the mass bitter alienation of men and women from the product of their labour, from society, from themselves, vast reserves of untapped talent, human beings hardly human. This we know can be ended in the generations of ourselves and our children and grandchildren, if the possibility is understood, and the effort made. This is not the *end*, but it is not a bad beginning to a real opening of *human, really human*, history.

Can we say then that Marxism is an eschatology? In the present context, this is, I think, for Christians to say. It is a Christian, not a Marxist, term, and whether Christians view our philosophy as eschatological or not, we shall not, I think, be unduly moved.

Changing Human Nature

When we as Marxists speak of the future society that we are confident can be achieved, we are apt to meet with, to put it mildly, a certain scepticism. It is interesting that from the Christian side we sometimes meet with the accusation that we are too pessimistic, too "materialist", for instance when we speak of rewards and incentives in a socialist society that has not yet reached the stage of communism. Equally the accusation is common that we are too (hopelessly, naively?) optimistic, discounting man's sinfulness and the "facts" of his Fall.

Often in different circles, we meet with that oft-repeated phrase "you can't change human nature", the most harmful, evil, reactionary phrase that can be combined out of six short words. Professor Pannenberg puts it in a much more sophisticated way (the Pannenberg problem it could well be called) when he poses the problem[13] of how can alienated man build, without divine intervention, an unalienated society?

In our opinion man is not born good or evil, he has neither "fallen", nor "risen", nor been redeemed. Man is both educated by and educates his environment. Men and women are constantly, ceaselessly changing.

There are two false views on changing human nature which are of interest to us in this discussion. One is often put in certain Christian

13 See p. 29 above.

circles, the other, alas, sometimes (quite wrongly) put in the name of Marxism. The first view is that *first* we must change man and *then* we will change society. The change is to come from outside, a sort of conversion. In its more displeasing form, I met it as a student at Cambridge when people used to come to us Communists, in the name of Moral Rearmament (then the Oxford Group of Buchmanites). "Look," they would say, "we have changed." No need for them to study, or act, or sacrifice, or show solidarity with the Hunger Marchers, or fight against war and fascism. They had "changed". Yet the more they told us about their spiritual "changing", the more we seemed to see their same old smug self-centred selves. There are far higher forms of this same approach, often deeply and sincerely held.

Equally wrong is the "vulgar" Marxist approach that "first we must change society, then we will change man". Many of us believed when we first became revolutionaries that all that would be necessary was for the working class to win political power and begin to change the economic structure of society, and all at once, almost instantaneously, you would have in all his glory, sinless and fully social, the new socialist man. This I now think is far from Marxism, nearer to utopianism. Those who think that you first change (or convert) man, and then he will build a bright new world, or that changing the economic structure of society automatically gives birth to a new people (though this is nearer to truth than the first postulate) are doomed to disillusion.

In all men and women, boys and girls (or at least in all who are not mentally sick) there is a vast potentiality, fantastic reserves, of infinitely varied capacity and talent. My political life has utterly sapped that old upper-class arrogance that the "swinish multitude" are fit only for simple tasks, of which the most important is to support their rulers and betters.

The most cruel aspect of the class society in which we live is that most working class people, and nearly all people in the Third "underdeveloped" World, have not the possibility to exercise more than a minute part of their potential capacity, and indeed most of them are left totally unaware of it. Yet in the last century, as the slumbering giant awakes, the working class movement and the national liberation struggles have shown something of that infinitely untapped capacity. How can that talent be released? Not in the main from outside or above. Not by charity or paternalism. Of course a communist society needs, and demands in order for it to operate, a new sort of man and woman, social in outlook, many-sided. But, in my opinion (and I believe this is the real Marxist view), men and women in struggle, binding themselves together in common

association, fighting to change external nature and society, continuously change themselves.

Communism needs new men and women. It is in the long, complex, uneven process of struggle against capitalism and imperialism, to bring about a revolutionary change in the social structure, building socialism, that men and women, step by step, painfully often, change themselves and fit themselves for a communist society.

With scarcity we hoard. This is true. If our chairman was suddenly to announce that in Birmingham this afternoon the shops were open and all was free and gratis, I doubt if even this distinguished theological audience could be held back. I have seen in the desert men long starved of water, coming upon it and drinking themselves sick. I saw in Yugoslavia, when liberation came from fascist occupation, men and women tearing open sacks of salt and cramming it into their mouths. But those who have long lived with limitless water do not leave the tap on.

This is the way to answer the Pannenberg problem. It is in the struggle to end an alienated society, to end their own alienation, that men and women will both achieve an unalienated society and fit themselves to live in it. Marxists see all things in their process of change: not only the cosmos, the earth, nature, society, thought, but also men and women and their characters.

Marx wrote:

> The whole of history is nothing but the progressive transformation of human nature. By acting on the world and changing it, man changes his own nature.[14]

Again he wrote in *Capital*:

> Man opposes himself to nature as one of her own forces. . . . By thus acting on the external world and changing it, he at the same time changes his own nature. He develops his slumbering powers and compels them to act in obedience to his will.[15]

Thinking of the future and the demands that the future society would make on man, he wrote, in *The Civil War in France*, of the French workers in the Paris Commune:

> The working class did not expect miracles from the Commune. They have no ready-made utopias to introduce *par decret du peuple*. They know that in order to work out their own emancipation, and along with it that higher form to which present society is irresistably tending through its own economic development, they will have to pass

[14] Karl Marx, *Poverty of Philosophy*.
[15] Karl Marx, *Capital*, vol. i, chapter 7, section 1.

through long struggles, through a series of historical processes, in the course of which men, no less than circumstances, will be completely transformed.[16]

It is fashionable sometimes today to counterpose the young and the old Marx. The young Marx is produced as the humanist, moralist, deeply concerned with man and his destiny. Against this is projected the image of an old "embittered" Marx concerned solely with crudely material economic problems and interested only in spreading the damnable doctrine of class struggle. This is a fantasy, ignorant at best, wantonly false at worst. There was a close logic in Marx's life and writings. True he turned first to the problems of man, his nature and his destiny. He wanted to free man from his aliena-tion. But he came to see that this demanded not only the revo-lutionary change of society from capitalism (which he analysed in detail) to socialism (which he saw in broad outline), but that this would be brought about by the struggle of the working class and its allies for the new society, in the course of which those involved would change themselves.

We can now restate the Marxist long-term aim, the basis of Marxist hope. We stand for and work for a world not only of plenty, but a world in which the infinitely varied human talents can be developed and exercised freely in each individual as part of a united human brotherhood. Our aim is not *just* production, the more effective production of goods. It is, above all, the free, all-round development of the individual personality. When Marx wrote in *Capital* of "the self-realization of the person", he explained that it was not merely "the method of adding to the efficiency of pro-ducing, but the method of producing fully developed human beings".

Before I proceed, let me say in passing that I was struck by a remark of the Bishop of Durham in discussion that one could at times perceive in the life and conduct of particular people, *or in a particular situation*, a sort of glimpse of the life to come. He spoke of an old and happy couple, a Darby and Joan. I must in my own context agree with this. It is easy enough for critics of socialism to produce examples of unethical, wrong, reactionary, criminal con-duct in this or that socialist country. We would not seek to dispute for a second that such occurs. If it did not, it would be a miracle, and incidentally disprove Marxism. But I have often in my own experience sensed, as it were, glints of the future—the fantastic honesty and morality of the Chinese guerrillas led by the Com-munists in the anti-Japanese war or in the liberated area around

16 Karl Marx, *The Civil War in France.* 1871.

Yenan, or amongst the Yugoslav Partisans fighting fascism. I have seen it in the deep human comradeship and solidarity of the workers in prolonged and bitter strikes, or in the sacrifices made in movements that were working illegally. I have seen and felt it in the course of residential communist schools. This too gives hope.

Science and Hope

We hope, and hoping work for a world where men and women can develop to the full their many talents, talents of creating, production, of art, affection and love, for a world where men and women can realize their human selves. This, not a million tons of this or cubic yards of that, is our deepest objective. But this does not in any way mean contempt for material production. On the contrary. There is an issue here that Marxists and Christians, within the context of their respective hopes, should deeply examine.

Speaking not so long ago at a Christian–Marxist dialogue held at Edinburgh University, I found a strong trend amongst some Christians in the audience to speak in opposition to, and in criticism of, the developments of modern science and technique. Some saw in them the bane of the modern world, the enemy of spiritual man, the negation of hope. On this Marxists feel very strongly. We see the enemy not in science and technique but, on the contrary, in the misuse and abuse of science and technique.

The most surface glance at the insufferable poverty of a vast area of the world—in India or Indonesia or the Arab lands or Africa or Latin America, let alone amongst the poorer sections of the population in the heart of Western capitalism (the Negroes of U.S.A. for example)—affords endless evidence of the need for *more* science and technique, *catering for their enormous needs.* We should not for a second, in my opinion, accept the myth of man's spiritual development, separate from, at the expense of, the fulfilment of his material needs. For a vast section of the population of the world, life is *not yet* human, *let alone* spiritual. It is half-animal, almost vegetable. Indeed, the very expectation of life is but a fraction of that which today is possible. Men and women are often old in their twenties and die in their thirties. What basis for spiritual life is thus afforded by this deprivation of science and technique? But, equally, Marxists do not accept the other myth that natural science and technological advance alone—in and for themselves—ensure progress and hope. We reject the "scientism" of the type of the technocrats or of the late H. G. Wells.

Science can destroy or construct; it can throw men out of work or give men leisure. The issue is under no circumstances the rejection

of that science which could rapidly give to the population of the world freedom from poverty, from insecurity—and from back-breaking, repetitious toil. The issue is: *Science—in whose hands? Science—for what purpose—for profit or the people? Science—for Man or Mammon?*

Our aim is the utmost development of science and technique, but science in the hands of the community itself (which in our opinion means socialism and then communism); eventually a world control of the use of science. In our view it is what Pope Paul's encyclical letter— *Populorum progressio*—calls the "international imperialism of money", that uses science for profit, and develops technique in such a way that millions of men and women are physically and mentally impoverished. But we believe that it is immoral (and often hypocritical) to praise man's spirituality whilst depriving him of his material needs. The rapid further development of technique and science, in the hands of the people, and used for their benefit, is an integral part of the Marxist hope.

Death and Immortality

Let me come back then to our discussion of hope—Christian hope and Marxist hope. We are often asked in all sincerity by many a Christian: "How can *you* speak of *hope*, when for you as atheists there is no life after death, when death is *final*, terminal, the *end?*" This seems to be a recurring theme in the Christian Testaments, Old and New. Dr Caird quoted "the rest of men who have no hope" (1 Thess. 4. 13), or the Gentiles "without God and without hope" (Eph. 2. 12), or "when death is certain and imminent hope ceases" (cf. Job 6. 11; 7. 6; 17. 15), or Paul in 1 Corinthians: "If it is for this life only that Christ has given us hope, we of all men are most to be pitied" (1 Cor. 15. 19). The old argument in endless anti-freethinker, anti-agnostic, anti-atheistic handbooks was the in-evitable immorality of the unbelievers "gathering rosebuds whilst they may", feckless in this world as they were heedless of the next.

Yet life, I think, has adequately shown the contrary. I was very moved at the National Christian–Marxist Dialogue held in St Katharine's, Stepney, in October 1967, when a Roman Catholic writer, Theo Westow, said that it seemed to be Communists who were most ready to die as martyrs for their beliefs in the world today. Indeed, as Sartre's character showed, Marxists seem so full of hope that it sometimes becomes to their fellows almost a re-proach.

The Marxist feels himself as an individual but also as part of society, or at least of what he considers the progressive part of society. He sees a deep distinction (which I have mentioned) be-

tween individualism and individuality. Individuality blossoms as part of the community, of the progressive classes in their struggle against reaction. The Marxist sees his future as part of his own effort with his fellows—his brothers, as the trade unionists say, or his comrades, as is our parlance in the Communist Party. Individuals, men and women, most effectively develop their talents, their potentialities, as part of the collective struggle. Isolation turning inwards leads often to despair. In effort, in struggle (class struggle in a class divided society) shared with his fellows, man finds hope.

Man comes to see his own self-realization in the collective. In doing this he, in a sense, transcends himself. The conception of solidarity is as old as the working class movement. A study of the Home Office papers of the early nineteenth century show letter after letter from indignant magistrates and local authorities to the Home Office deploring precisely this qualilty—making "common cause"[17] (the Leeds magistrate Cookson in 1801) "unfortunately true to each other,"[18] (Lord Pembroke to Home Office). "One out, all out" has always been the slogan of the dockers.

Coming back to the point, a Marxist feels identified with the common struggle even when as an individual he knows that he may not or will not see the end of it; yes, even when death is involved.

In one sense it is particularly hard for a Marxist to face death—there is so much to do, so much to live for. But in another sense he finds it perhaps easier to look death in the eyes, for as an individual he lives on in the class and community in struggle, and he has left his mark on it and contributed to it. Man is mortal, mankind immortal.

Of course Marxists, too, know fears, hesitations, and tribulations. But in the last analysis communist hope transcends individual hope. We hope to make life as long and sweet, rewarding and fulfilling, as we can, and so to work that dying we can say: "In this way we have contributed to the future of our fellow man, and in them we will live on." Then even death is not without hope. At a communist funeral we like to celebrate all that he who is dead has done for the common cause. The ceremony is without ritual, informal. But often we read the words from the novel of the Soviet Young Communist, Nikolai Ostrovsky—*How Steel Was Tempered*—who at fifteen, fighing in the civil war, was badly wounded, later lost his sight, and was completely paralysed; he lay in his bed till his death at the age of thirty-two, but never lost heart. Blind and paralysed he wrote this book about another young Communist, Pavel Korchagin.

---

[17] H.O. 42. 66.
[18] Ibid.

Pavel returns one day to the spot where his young comrades had been hanged in the civil war:

> On this spot Pavel's comrades had gone bravely to their deaths that life might be beautiful for those born in poverty. . . . Slowly Pavel raised his hand and removed his cap, his heart filled with sadness.

> Man's dearest possession is life. It is given to him but once, and he must live it so as to feel no torturing regret for wasted years, never know the burning shame of a mean and petty past; so live that, dying, he might say: all my life, all my strength, were given to the finest cause in all the world—the fight for the Liberation of Mankind.

Marxist Hope

To sum up. For Marxists, hope is a lived relation to reality expressed psychologically, politically, philosophically. Basing themselves on what they see as necessary, possible, and achievable for humanity, or for a patricular section of it, at a given stage of the development of science and of man, they *hope* for its accomplishment. But the future demands effort, sacrifice, struggle. It is not "ordained", "written", "predetermined" by God nor by genes, by geography nor even by economic development. Men make their own history, within the limits of what they have inherited from the past.

So Marxist hope—hope for socialism and communism, for a world without hunger and war, for a world of brotherhood, a world where each man and woman can develop fully his or her many-sided talents as part of the community—is based on the understanding that all of those must be achieved, in effort and struggle, by men. The very hope spurs on the hoper to action, the very action gives strength to the hope. The Marxist hope is a goal of action; a conviction that what is hoped for can be realized, that one can contribute to its accomplishment.

Such is our hope for preventing a third World War and of one day ending war for ever. Such is our hope of ending the American aggression in Vietnam. Such is the hope that has strengthened revolutionaries in situations that seemed despairing—in fascist concentration camps, conditions of colonialist domination, in the hunger of unemployment, in the last defiant shout of an executed guerrilla soldier, or in the dignified death of one incurably ill.

We live at a moment of formidable revolt of the youth (including students of theology). Some of that revolt is above all negative—against the establishment, its cruelty, its wars, imperialist oppression, colonialism, against its commercialized culture and moral hypocrisy. But protest *against*, alone, gives only a short-lived hope. Real hope comes when there is a sense of objective, of replacing what is old and bad, rotting and rotten, with something that is new

and better, that is coming into being, that *can* be built, that represents the future.

The great hope of youth is to pass from revolt and rebellion *against*, disgust *with*, wanting to opt *out of*, refusing to accept responsibility *for*, to the fight *for* a new society and a new world. Negative revolt can start with hope, but unless it is transformed from rebellion *against* into revolution *for*, the hope can become resignation and hopelessness. Real hope demands the transition from rebel to revolutionary. Hence the importance of Marxism.

It must not be thought that all the life of all of us who consider ourselves Marxists is at the level of which I have been speaking. Becoming a communist is a life-time task. At other levels we *hope* to win the pools, we hope that our tumour will not be malignant, we hope that tomorrow the sun will shine. Marxists too have their moments of anguish, temptation, and, at times, of betrayal. But I have tried to put in relief the essence of the Marxist hope, to show that it is not an escape from the ugliness of life, not an act of despair, not an odd, occasional, or selfish desire, not a promise of reward, but a confidence that better things can be achieved now and in the future by men's struggle and action, including ours, that though the achievements of our aims is never certain, it is possible and should be attempted.

Christian Hope and Marxist Hope

I have read attentively the previous chapters in this book. There was much that I cannot share and much that I found difficult to comprehend. Clearly there are some deep differences between us. But we must perforce ask whether, within our mutual hopes, there are not points of contact, zones that we can share. I must ask in all sincerity, how far is Christian hope confined to life after death, eternal life after the resurrection, and how far in a new understanding of the present? It seems to me that this has not been sufficiently touched on, and this is a question asked not just by Marxists and non-believers, but by millions of committed Christians throughout the world, particularly by Christian youth. Dr Caird posed the question, but did little more than hint at the reply.

May I, to the Pannenberg problem, counter-pose the Klugmann question? Is Christian hope something to be, through faith, *awaited*, or something through which men and women in their efforts *now* have a part to play? Borrowing the words of the Reverend Anthony Dyson (writing on Teilhard de Chardin:[19] Is Christ for a Christian

---

[19] See Paul Oestreicher and James Klugmann, ed., *What Sort of Revolution?* (Panther paperback 1968).

an "external agent compelling a static, passive humanity towards its destiny" or "a stimulus assisting a process from within, an influence to which man may or may not respond"? Does God, in the eyes of a Christian, standing before man as a measure of his possibility "beckon to him to enter and change it and build this earth as the necessary precondition for his own final act of consummation"? Does Christian hope include the acceptance of a responsibility to act now to improve society and men, and does it see any connection between this and the world to come? This is the question I feel impelled to ask. Perhaps I put it in clumsy non-theological words, but to me the answer is very important.

I *hope* that Marxists and Christians within their mutual hopes can find a measure of common ground. And when I say I *hope*, I am using the word in a Marxist sense. I believe that there *is* such common ground, and that within large areas of the Marxist and Christian communities men and women will work to make this true. And hoping thus I will personally accept a share in the responsibility for helping to bring it about.

5

IMMORTALITY AND
LIFE AFTER DEATH

NINIAN SMART

THE approach to the problem of immortality adopted in this paper is primarily phenomenological. The reason for this is that it is unwise to introduce philosophical arguments for the conceptual possibility of survival after death or of resurrection of the body without placing the question in the context of religion and religious life. Besides, the viability of some notion of survival has already been sufficiently brought out in recent discussions.[1] On the other hand, it is not necessarily illuminating to consider the problem through an exposition of the Christian theology of death (whatever that may be). Rather I wish to place the problem in a wider phenomenological context, and thereby to try to illuminate some of the features of the Christian faith and to exhibit some options open to the Christian theologian in the further exploration of the meaning of immortality and resurrection.

One indeed feels the artificiality and degeneration implicit in efforts to produce speculative and quasi-scientific arguments to back up belief in survival. To produce a certain sort of argument for survival is by implication to interpret that belief in a certain way. I am not saying that the question whether, say, disembodied persons continue individual existence beyond the grave is unimportant; but in the context of psychical research such evidence as there might be would be more crucial for the biological sciences than for the interpretation of mythic faith in immortality. Somehow the mythic faith seems to have degenerated when we get down to speculative arguments and spiritualistic evidences. The reason, perhaps, why there is a nisus towards such speculation on the part of the Christian

[1] See, for instance, Stewart R. Sutherland, "Immortality and Resurrection" in *Religious Studies*, vol. 3, no. 1 (1967); also H. H. Price, "The Problem of Life after Death", ibid., vol. 3, no. 2 (1968). Further, P. F. Strawson, *Individuals*, ch. 6.

theologian or philosopher is that we *want* to treat the myths as somehow literal. On the other hand, we also want to see immortality and the resurrection of the body as symbolical of the conquest of death. The myth has to be both literal and metaphorical. It is in a way both; but also it is neither. We have slit the fish in two, yet we still wish it to swim. What then is to be done? I shall try to start further back, by examining some of the principles of religious thinking and feeling.

In the ensuing I shall use the term "god" to refer either to God or to the gods. This may be thought to gloss over the question of the uniqueness of God in the Christian tradition, etc.; but I shall return to that point in the conclusion.

Some Remarks on the Myths of Immortality

Immortality is often thought of as a characteristic of god; and myth is replete with stories of how men have forfeited immortality either by loss of it or by failure to grasp it when craftily offered by god. Consider the following story from Indonesia :[2]

> Thus the natives of Poso, a district of central Celebes, say that in the beginning the sky was very near the earth, and that the Creator, who lived in it, used to let down his gifts to men at the end of a rope. One day he thus lowered a stone; but our first father and mother would have none of it, and they called out to their Maker, "What have we to do with this stone? Give us something else.". . . Presently the rope was seen coming down from heaven again, and this time there was a banana at the end of it instead of a stone. Our first parents ran at the banana and took it. Then there came a voice from heaven saying: "Because ye have chosen the banana, your life shall be like its life. When the banana-tree has offspring, the parent stem dies; so shall ye die and your children shall step into your place. Had ye chosen the stone, your life would have been like the life of the stone, changeless and immortal." The man and his wife mourned over their fatal choice, but it was too late; that is how through the eating of a banana, death came into the world.

Two incidental features of this myth are worth noting, for they bear on the phenomenological analysis I shall be undertaking. First, there is the notion that once the distance between heaven and earth was less. This hints at a state where alienation from god is not great —where, so to say, the psychological distance between god and man is less than now. Second, you become like what you participate in (for example, what you eat); this root idea is, as we shall see, very important in the relations of god and man. However, the main

2 M. Eliade, ed., *From Primitives to Zen* (1967), p. 140, quoting J. G. Frazer and A. C. Kruijt.

meaning of the story is that men have put aside, admittedly un-knowingly, a divine gift of immortality.

Typically, death is regarded as a crucial existential problem, and so deathlessness as an attribute of god is coveted, aspired to, by man. But the lethal suggestion of many myths is that god is jealous, and will not have man pretending to claim god's attributes for himself. In the Indonesian myth, god offers immortality, for in the end god is gracious; but craftily he does not tell man of the real nature of the gift. Does such guile make sense? It does, once we dig deeper into the phenomenology of god–man relationships, and of the nature of godhood. This phenomenology I wish to sketch by citing a number of principles.

The Principle of Dynamism:
God is both Personal Entity and Divisible Substance

God is more than a personal being and focus of worship, for his power can flow forth and operate in a semi-autonomous fashion. Such power can be personalized, as in the iconography of Śakti as the female consort of god in the Indian tradition; or it can be impersonal, substance-like power, as when god's attributes are hypostatized or become immanent dynamic forces within the created order. Thus, in the *Bhagavadgītā* there is the passage:

> I am the taste in water . . . ; I am the light in the moon and sun; I am AUM in the Vedas; I am sound in air, and personhood in men (vii. 8).

For this reason there is often a fluidity in the notion of identity with god; and in any event the criteria of identity as beween putatively different entities in religion are somewhat different from those applicable in more mundane contexts.[3] Sometimes a distinction is made between sharing in the divine divisible substance and achieving actual identity with god. This is divinization through sharing god's attributes but not his essence (to advert to a quasi-philosophical contrast useful in guarding theism from becoming confused with monism).

The Principle of Humility before Godhood

Godhood is intrinsically holy, and god is typically focus of worship.[4] Thus there is always some numinous distance between god and man, sometimes symbolized by the distance between heaven and earth.

---

[3] See my "Criteria of Religious Identity", *Philosophical Quarterly*, vol. 8 (1958).
[4] Typically, not always; for there can be the *deus otiosus*, too high to con-cern himself with men; also there can be the gods who are transcended by nirvana, *Tīrthaṁkaras*, etc., in Buddhism and Jainism—they tend to fade as objects of public cultus.

However, the exaltation of godhood and the corresponding humility of man before god is a matter of degree, for it depends on the context in which god is placed as well as on the numinous power god displays. The situation varies according to whether godhood is treated as singular or plural, supreme or provisional. Thus in some religions there are many gods, and in so far as they jostle together in the realm of the numinous, none may attain utterly exalted status. Again the gods may be transcended by nirvana or godhood may be regarded as provisional, as in Advaita Vedanta—a lower manifestation of a supreme but impersonal Absolute.[5] Sometimes the exaltation of god may lead to his losing living contact with man, since man by the principle of humility may consider his daily concerns to be too trivial for the high god, and so address himself more existentially to lesser, nearer spirits (this is, for example, in some cultures the function of the saints). But let us treat the simplest, and from the point of view of the Judaeo-Christian-Islamic complex, the most crucial, case of godhood—where there is but one supreme god, focus of worship and devotion. (But we may note in passing that there is a closely analogous case in, for example, Vaiṣṇavism : for Rāmānuja the lower gods are part of the divisible substance of the one supreme Lord.)

Because god is supremely holy, the proper worship of god is the ascription, that is, recognition and acceptance, of his supreme holiness. But since god, by the principle of dynamism, floats, even when highly personalized, ambivalently between personal entity and substantive power, the uniqueness of god implies the uniqueness of his holy power. That is to say, there is no holy power outside god, just as there is no god outside god. Hence in addressing god as supremely and uniquely holy, the worshipper necessarily sees himself as without holy power of his own; and in so far as god is exalted, the worshipper is abased. This is the great phenomenological distance between heaven and earth.

The Principle of Grace

It follows from the principle of dynamism that god's attributes and powers can be, as it were, conferred on the created order. It is thus not absurd for man to look for participation in divine immortality, to overcome his own mortality. Yet is it not impious to seek a share in godhood, to participate in the divine substance? It seems that godhood acts by attraction and repulsion. In coming into contact with godhood, man sees its glory and power, and wants to share in

5 For a categorization of the cases, see my *Doctrine and Argument in Indian Philosophy* (1964), pp. 214-16.

it. But the greater the power and the glory, the greater the phenomenological inconsistency in seeking for it. It is out of this situation that the principle of humility can come to have a compound force. By seeking the glory of godhood, man becomes blasphemous and impious; in becoming impious, he becomes alienated from godhood. This alienation is not just lack of contact with godhood; it is not mere absence of some attribute; but it is more radically an experience of the wrath of god—a fall. (A gentle version of this alienation was contained in the Indonesian myth earlier quoted.) Thus the principle of the proper humility of man before the supreme focus of worship is reinforced by the natural alienation of man from god by the operation of the dynamics of attraction and repulsion in godhood's relation to man.

The necessary humility and alienation of man before the glory and power of god results, where the focus of worship is supreme, in a radical phenomenology of grace. Godhood can impart something of its own substance; but this can only be by the operation of godhood, not by the works or power of anything outside godhood. This conception naturally fits with a certain view of creation—namely that everything in the cosmos is dependent upon God's power; and even if secondary causes have to be admitted, they remain as semi-detached forces based on the power of god.

If, then, man is to participate in the divine substance, it is through the operation of god as having the initiative and as sole possessor and originator of holiness. The principle of grace can of course be applied in a variety of forms—in the predestinationism of Islam and of Calvinism, in Rāmānuja's Vaisnavism, in the fideism of Pure Land Buddhism, in the offering by God of a Covenant, etc. It can manifest itself in various guises—through the impartation of godhood sacramentally, for instance. In so far as the idea of God is given ethical content ,the principles of grace and humility can have divers moral by-products—in moral humility, in the god-given brotherhood of men before god, in the sense of gracious egalitarianism (i.e. that god is no respecter of social status in his free self-giving to those who have faith).

The Principle of Participation

It has been assumed in much of this discussion of the phenomenology of the numinous focus of worship that the typical result of contact between man and god is either the participation of man in something of the divine substance or positive alienation therefrom (we might call this participation in anti-godhood). There is, of course, a question of what contact amounts to, and to this I shall turn shortly. By participation is meant something like this. If *ps* are the

powers and properties of x, then y participates in x when and only when he acquires some p; and that p which y acquires is a portion of the divisible substance of p. The principle of humility would imply that y could not acquire all the ps of god, for then y would become god; and this would be impossible since god would no longer be focus of worship, etc. But of course the principle of humility might not be an overriding consideration. Thus in Advaita Vedānta the worshipper is at a higher level actually identical with Brahman—so that the principle of humility could at best only have provisional significance. However, where the principle of humility before godhood is fully operational, that is, where there is a supreme focus of worship, there is a limit on participation, since the idea of identity with godhood would be ruled out, and so there remains a dialectical tension between the otherness of godhood and the possibility of human participation in the powers and properties of godhood. This tension is resolved if all the sharing of properties occurs through the initiative of godhood.

Further, it may turn out that the properties and powers attained by men in virtue of their participation in godhood are partly or wholly analogical, in virtue of the way in which simultaneously men are and are not sharers in godhood. For instance, the mythic idea of man's being made in the image of god suggests that god has creatively imprinted an analogue of his own powers on the creature. The myth of the Fall, however, goes further in suggesting not merely that man remains creaturely before God but also that, by participation in anti-godhood, man has obscured the powers formerly analogically enjoyed by him, so that there exists an even more powerful tension which only god can overcome by the self-impartation of further powers—ones which enable men more fully, despite the alienation, to participate in the divine life.

The question of the nature of contact needs, however, to be explored; for this is an element in the situation of attraction and repulsion which can lead to alienation. There are multiple ways in which such contact can be manifested. It is, for instance, a constantly reiterated theme in the *Upaniṣads* that knowledge or gnosis of Brahman brings the powers of Brahman, or some of them, to the one who knows. Thus knowledge of god, very often somewhat indirectly, can count as a form of contact; Paul in Romans (1. 19-21) was thus able to argue that pagans knew something of the true god but turned away towards idolatry. Most dramatically, the numinous experience of the one god is a form of contact; not surprisingly it brings home man's humility and alienation.[6] Or it may be that

---

[6] As in Job, and in the calls of Isaiah and Jeremiah.

godhood is disguised at the point of contact—for example, through the eucharistic sacrament or through the re-presentation of godhood in the kerygma. In the one case there is the possibility of sharing the divisible substance of godhood or of eating and drinking to damnation; in the other, there is the response of faith (enabling one to share Christ's life) or the response of rejection. Again, contact may be conceived as mediated by the divine Law (a situation encouraged by the ethical attributes woven into the holiness of godhood in ethical monotheism)—so that participation in god's holiness may come by acceding to his Law (or alternatively alienation may come either through rebelling against the Law or through attempting, by moral goodness, to generate a man-made holiness).

Some Further Remarks on Immortality

The application of the foregoing to the problem of immortality is as follows. First, immortality is a crucial divine property (though we shall later have to inquire precisely why this is so). Second, man's quest for immortality is impious; for he is trying to generate godhood on his own—but this is incompatible with a supreme holy focus of worship. Third, in so far as the doctrine of an immortal soul may be held to assign intrinsic immortality to man, it is incompatible with the phenomenology of worship. Man gains immortality only by the self-apportioning to him of this divine attribute (or, alternatively, alienated man may be assigned the super-death of hell, the ultimate participation in anti-godhood). The concept of the resurrection of the body has built into it the idea of divine action, whereas the idea of the immortality of the soul does not. However, the latter is compatible with the idea of the divine provenance of immortality.

There are, in the field of religions, other pictures. Thus the idea of rebirth may be fitted to the phenomenology of theistic worship by seeing rebirth as the mode under which the karmic power of God works out human destiny, as in Rāmānuja's theology and that of Madhva. Here, in a way, the impartation of part of the divine substance to individuals involves the overcoming of a kind of immortality, that is, the otherwise perpetual rebirth and redeath of individuals. Eternal life is figured as transcending literal immortality. But it is interesting to note that the theistic phenomenology drives Rāmānuja to postulate God as the gracious inner-controller within the individual, and to see *karma* as a divine operation. Thus the autonomous soul, intrinsic to living beings, is no longer autonomous or intrinsic to living beings; but something essentially imparted to creatures out of the divisible substance of the one Lord.

*The Myth of Christ and some Elements in it
which are Foci of Participation*

Immortality in the Christian tradition has, obviously, to be related
above all to the myth of Christ, to the life, death, and resurrection
of Christ. This is the particular historical form in which the dialectical tension in man's relation to godhead is resolved. This tension is
acute in the Christian treatment because of the strong emphasis
placed by the Christian tradition on the myth of alienation. This is
the obverse of God's act of atonement and redemption—the closing
of the alienating gap between God and man. In so far as man, in
recognition of his sin and alienation from the supreme focus of his
worship, strives to do something about that alienation, to expiate
his sin, he must fail. The principle of humility seems to make room
for such an effort of expiation, and it is therefore easy for man to be
impelled in this direction, without at first noting the inconsistency
of this course. It must be inconsistent, for he must by the same
principle recognize that only god can impart the holiness which
expiation might bring. The trouble is compounded by man's
necessary alienation from an ethical god, for goodness itself is both
now an offshoot of the divine divisible substance and in human
terms impossible of perfect fulfilment. Numinous and ethical sin
are conflated in one obstinate package. Only man can expiate his
sin; but only godhood can impart holiness. Thus there is a certain
phenomenological logic in the idea of god's incarnation. The god-
man saves and expiates in one gracious movement. There are other
motifs too in the myth which blend with the foregoing. The
humanity of the saviour is maintained by the way in which godhood imparts itself in disguise, as in a sacrament—or perhaps one
should say *incognito*. Yet in this mysterious form the theoretical
limit of self-impartation is reached, for it is god's inner personhood
that is imparted, i.e. the god-man actually is identical with god (such
an identity, however, does not entail anything about god-conscious-
ness, etc.).

But the phenomenological logic is only a framework. Every
instantiation of godhood has its particular form, and the particular
form of godhood in the Christian tradition is necessarily tied to the
particularities of the myth of Christ. There is of course some
question as to what should be taken to be part of the myth of Christ.
Let us here treat only of ways in which the Christian might participate in Christ's death and resurrection, by reference to the foci of
such participation and by reference to the sacramental vehicle
through which participation in Christ occurs.

Christ's death can be seen in one perspective as a moral act, and

one presumably surrounded by despair. Christ as *man* died. Since, however, the divine and human sides of the myth are inextricably fused, so long as the myth remains myth and is not cut in two so that it can no more swim amongst us, there is a sense in which the Christian can participate in that death. But in an ordinary way, participation in Christ's human death is a moral analogy—that the Christian can through the self-impartation of godhood gain the moral style of Jesus in his way of self-sacrifice and despairing faith. What is it, though, to participate in the divine side of Christ's death? The latter is the saving act which removes essentially the alienation between godhood and man; and works by grace and expiation simultaneously. This is partaken of by the Christian, in the sense that sacramentally he realizes relationship with godhood hitherto blocked by his alienation. But does such non-alienated contact with the divine substance give the Christian eternal life, immortality? It should be so: for immortality is a typical power and property of godhood, and godhood is typically self-imparting, when there is no repulsion. But the place of immortality has to be seen in its relation- ship to the firmament of values.

Death and the Firmament of Values

Death sometimes appears in the guise of a threat to our values, a symbol of the meaninglessness of human endeavour. But what does "meaning" mean in such a context? When someone says that his life has no meaning any more, or that his job does not mean anything to him any more, etc., he is, I think, drawing attention to the decay or diminution of values. That is, activities once valuable-for-him no longer seem important, enjoyable, etc. Conversely, life is meaningful in proportion to the values capable of being realized in it. Further, there is a way in which the conservation or expansion of values is future-oriented; for usually what is valuable-for-us is woven in- extricably into a fabric of ongoing institutions and projects. This is one reason for the asymmetry of group or individual attitudes to future non-existence as compared with attitudes to past non- existence. Thus the thought that there might be a day when there is no cricket played any more is more harrowing than the thought that there once was a day when there was no cricket. This future- orientation gives rise to a sense of hopelessness if we contemplate universal destruction; a modern sense of this is found in Nevile Shute's ghastly tale *On the Beach*. Likewise, when a group has its institutions shattered by external forces, the members of the group can go into a kind of *accidie* and numb despair; hence the rise too of new cults to restore or create values and expand the life

of the group.[7] A sense of the vertigo induced by the thought of destruction also assails us when we contemplate buried civilizations —stone monuments to whole ways of life vanished now. In a way the destruction of the group is much more poignant than that of the individual. The latter shared his life and values with others, and those values continue in chains of lives linked with his. His own intrinsic value can no longer be realized in his acts and smiles and tears; but it lives on in some form, in the ancestral tablet and in the rituals of memory. But if these are wiped out and the group obliterated, it is as though he had never been.

The firmament of values of an individual or group is liable to accept godhood as an overarching value. The focus of worship in its dynamism and numinous power naturally expands to become a superarching value. By the principle of dynamism the divine substance suffuses and comprehends customs and morality; and by the principle of humility man comes to subordinate his values to the intrinsic holiness (now including goodness) of the personalized godhood.[8] The values realized here on earth are perceived as a gift of god, and morality as command. As godhood comes to occupy the central place in the firmament of values, and as it becomes the supreme source of values, it acquires a certain "absoluteness". This absoluteness amounts to the unshakeableness of its intrinsic value, as contrasted with the values achieved by humans and with the value of humans themselves.

A bridge conception which spans the distance between god seen as focus of worship and god seen as source of values is the idea of creation. The phenomenology of worship here suggests a certain ontology. By the principle of humility god and man are not to be identified; so likewise the created order in which man swims is other from god, though suffused by his dynamic power (the created order therefore is good). The distinction between world and godhood tends therefore to carry with it a sense of the *reality* of the world, which spills over, as it were, into an attitude of this-worldliness to offset the ineluctable other-worldliness of worship focused on transcendent godhood. Where, incidentally, man is regarded as having by presumptuous contact with godhood become alienated or fallen, it is a natural transition to think of the created order as a whole as having fallen. It is ontologically real, but valuationally vitiated.

The distinct reality of man creates, however, a phenomenological tension when it comes to the problem of participation in the im-

7 See, for example, V. Lanternari, *Religions of the Oppressed* (1963).

8 A more formal exposition of this point is to be found in my "Gods, Bliss and Morality", reprinted in Ian Ramsey, ed., *Christian Ethics and Contemporary Philosophy* (1966).

mortality of god. If god's absolute value is unshakeable, man can perhaps hope that his non-alienated contact with god will ensure that his own values are divinized and so made similarly unshakeable. The symbol of this unshakeability is eschatological—given the future-orientation of human values to which I have referred. But is this future conservation of values to be conceived as the transfer of man—of the individual, group, or mankind as a whole—to a heaven close to godhood? Or is it to be conceived as a transformation and re-creation of the created order? More particularly: immortality of the soul or resurrection of the body? Here the tension is not so much to do with the principle of grace (i.e. to do with the question of whether man's holy immortality is intrinsic to him or rather given by the goodness of godhood). It is to do with the locus of immortality—whether its locus is transcendental or of this world. The polarity of other-world and this-world crosses with the polarity of individual and group. This yields some different conceptions of the eschatological participation in the immortality of the divine substance.

Some Types of Eschatology

These polarities yield four theoretical types of eschatology, within the general framework of the phenomenology of worship. The first theoretical case is the re-creation of the individual, but not of the collective, in this world. The second type, namely a future con-summation of the group's values and projects, has its mythic formulation in the eschatology of the Second Coming in the early Church and has a more recent expression in the evolutionary myth of Teilhard de Chardin, culminating in the Omega point. The third theoretical type is the notion of the transcendental immortality of the individual close to the power and glory of godhood. Fourthly, there is the idea of the collective realization of transcendental immortality in the communion of saints, etc. (But in addition one would have to consider the sea-change made to the classification by taking rebirth into account.) Now it could be said, by the principle of grace, that whichever of these futures is actual is due to the unilateral decision of godhood. But since for the Christian the essential datum is the myth of Christ, it is useful to consider what would seem to follow—given this datum—within the framework of the phenomenology of participation. For we have seen that the death and resurrection of Christ form foci of participation in him, via his sacramental life. The first thing to notice is the temporal relation of Christ's death and resurrection—the one is definitely *after* the other (this is doubtless in accord with the sense of

historical sequence so prominent in the Jewish tradition to which Christ belonged). But here we meet the phenomenological problems of the relations between past, present, and future which meets us when the axis of time is crossed by the axis of holy otherness.

Past, Present, and Future,
from the point of view of Participation in Godhood
and of the Immortalizing of Human Values

Any god, operating through a past event, can confer some of his divine substance not only on the past event but on the human values traced back to that event (hence, for example, the validation of the Sabbath in the Genesis myth); participation here is, so to say, transitive. The present practice has its archetype in the original event—so that the sanctification of the past event sanctifies what is present as a recurrent custom. The nexus between present and past is of course much stronger when there is an explicit sacramental connection. Thus Christ's death and resurrection themselves are present sacramentally to Christians now. Just as the past becomes present, so can the future be anticipated. Since godhood is ever-lasting, timeless, immortal, spanning past, present, and future, it can give not only of its present substance (for example, through faith-experience) or of its past value-conferring substance, but also of its future substance. In the case of the Christian tradition, participation in the victorious cross points forward in time to participation in the resurrection. Further, the logic of the Christian community, united by participation in Christ and in the sense of being a renewed group (Israel) in relation to godhood, suggests that participation in the future conferral of the unshakeability of value by godhood is a communal matter, doubtless universal to mankind. However, it is difficult to distinguish this hope of the future partici-pation in the divisible immortal substance of godhood, justifying and consummating the ongoing values and projects of humanity, from the present participation in the transcendent. But in knowing the risen Christ here and now we are participating both in death and in the temporally sequential resurrection. In gaining, through the principle of grace, the benefit accruing upon Christ's sacrificial death, we participate in the immortal godhood; and we look forward from that vantage-point to the consummation of his and our lives. However, from the point of view of the immortalizing of human values, through the over-arching supreme focus of worship's grace-ful self-impartation of value in the direction of our human values and so aspirations, the future counts more than the past or even the present. Hence the stress which we may want to lay upon the

future immortalization of our projects, at the end of history—as it is said.

Since also Christ was human, participation in his glory tends in the direction of a this-worldly consummation, even if the phenomenology of worshp impels folk towards a heavenly, transcendental, focus of the divinized life of the individual and of the community. It is an illustration of the ding-dong pendulum between the divine side of the Christ myth and the human side; and more generally between the symbolic and the literal in myth (fused together, as we have seen, despite attempts to slit the fish in two). In any event, the emphasis in the logic of participation in the mythic Christ is towards the future and this world. But woe unto those who split the myth and try to specify some future evolutionary state corresponding to the general resurrection or to the Second Coming. Nor can Christ be divorced, in the phenomenology of worship, from the figure of the transcendent personalized god, from whom alienation occurred and therefore the *felix culpa* resulting in the death and resurrection of Christ.

The net result of the principle of participation as applied to the temporal sequence of Christ's saving work is that contact with godhood in the guise of Christ can bring redemption and the divinization of human values and projects. Since men can participate in the divine substance now, they thereby participate in the future consummation. But it is, of course, hard to say what that concretely means. Assume that in death Christ could not see forward to the resurrection; and you can then assume that we, in participating in Christ, have no foreknowledge of the future consummation and immortalization of human values.

Some Concluding Remarks arising from the Foregoing

I have attempted to illustrate the phenomenological logic of worship, and to relate that to the mythic datum of Christ's life, death, and resurrection. It would be possible at first sight for the secularizing modern Christian theologian to resist this kind of description of the phenomenology from various points of view. All of them are inadequate; so that what I have written is in essence a challenge to them.

First, it is no good arguing that I have been trying to bring out the logic of *religious* phenomenology, while the Christian gospel (i.e. Christ *in concreto*) essentially transcends religion. This honest ploy does not work, since, firstly, other religions can work the same self-critical, self-transcending gambit (and have done so—for example, Nāgārjuna in Buddhism—the essential *dharma* transcends the empirical *dharma*, etc.); and secondly, either the transcending

gospel is continuous with Judaeo-Christian religious life or it is not; if it is, then it is a self-critical, deep version, but if it is not, then it has no logical connection with the Church or with Christ.[9]

Second, anyone who tries to restate the essence of Christianity without reference to the personalized numinous godhood and to the sacramental Christ must abandon the principles of dynamism, humility, grace, and participation. Above all, he must reject the very idea of grace in presenting a non-numinous kerygma. It is absurd to present Christ without god, unless one rejects the phenomenological logic of god.

Third, the motifs I have sketched are not unique to the Judaeo-Christian, though certainly the myth of Christ is; one can therefore either take the radical turn by jettisoning the phenomenology of godhood, worship, and sacrament; or one can recognize that the framework round the Christ-myth has its echoes (to put it mildly) in other faiths. The former course points to a new humanism; the second course points to some kind of rejection of exclusivism.

[9] See my "The Comparative Study of Religion" in D. Jenkins, ed., *The Scope of Theology* (1965).

6

NEW HEAVENS AND
A NEW EARTH?

W. A. WHITEHOUSE

God's purpose for the physical universe is for the most part hidden from us in mystery; we do not suppose that its only function is to provide support and discipline for men's bodies and minds during their lifetime on earth. We are certain that God's purpose will be worthy of his own majesty, and that it will be consistent with the dignity and splendour apparent in the universe to minds instructed through scientific enquiry. Yet we do not know, either in Christian faith or through scientific enquiry, what God will do with his creation when he completees the open expression of his sovereignty...

We look forward to acts of God which bring final transformation to human life and admit human beings to share in his own eternal joy and felicity. Creatures have been called into being to reflect the uninmaginable glory of the everlasting God. Cleansed from sin we shall see God in Jesus Christ in open splendour, and he will make us like himself. We do not know in what universal framework human lives so transfigured will be set; nor how in that framework God's other purposes for his created universe will be fulfilled. We do know that God is the source, the guide and the goal of all that is, and that in his serenity he sees the end from the beginning.[1]

Taught by Immanuel Kant, modern men find it hard to declare confidence in God until they are satisfied that what they say accords with some "Critique of Pure Theological Reason".[2] Human speech

[1] *A Declaration of Faith, adopted by the Congregational Church in England and Wales*. Published in London by Independent Press Ltd, 1967. The passages are paras. 1 and 6 from Section VI: "God will triumph".
[2] Modern theologians provide as best they can their own account of being and knowing. When Karl Heim produced the theology which eventually made him rank as an outstanding modern authority in the field which I am exploring, he set up the elaborate framework of "polarities" by way of preface in *God Transcendent* (Nisbet 1936). Karl Rahner clears the ground in another way in *The Theology of Death* (Herder: Burns & Oates 1961). My

expresses the awareness of human beings, physically constituted for life in a physically constituted universe. It is speech disciplined by reflection and argument, serving to clarify that with which they deal and which deals with them, and serving also to clarify the terms on which these dealings take place. Among much which, at first sight, merely "happens", men regard themselves as "agents" whose "activity" provides the kind of "actuality" in which they can have a rational interest. They ask, critically, whether this agency-language can be applied more widely, and if so with what distinctions. It is applied, in the passages cited, to "acts of God". Human awareness has produced traditions about "God". They are traditions which suggest that human living is open towards an unseen Lord, towards an unseen future, and towards enigmatic fellow-creatures. Supported by these traditions men conduct their lives by faith working through love with hope in God. Christian men speak in their faith about "what no eye has seen, nor ear heard, nor the heart of man conceived, which God has prepared for those who love him"; and this, they claim, "God has revealed to us through the Spirit" (1 Cor. 2. 6-10).

What prospect have they glimpsed? Life is theirs at present within a physical universe of which they are part. Appearances suggest that physical fact is infested with built-in obsolescence. Physical entities wear out, and wear one another out. Is the prospect of ever-renewed splendour, unmarred by any taint of wearing-out, compatible with the form of being known to us as spatio-temporal physicality? "We do not know, either in Christian faith or through scientific inquiry, what God will do with his creation when he completes the open expression of his sovereignty." Yet in worship men have seen fit to express what they hope for; and in theology "which proclaims the glory of Christ in the name of God, and develops the proclamation in the realm of thought"[3] they have discussed the reasonable warrant for doing so.

Our obligation is to develop a theology appropriate for men whose own knowledge of the world and of themselves has been acquired by experience, men who also believe that they and their world are *known by God*. We do it within a tradition where God is revered as Creator of heaven and earth and of all things visible and invisible.

crude observations on method in sections I and V represent what I have derived, unsystematically, from two theologians whom I most respect: (Edmund Schlink, *The Coming Christ and the Coming Church* (Oliver & Boyd 1966), Part 1, ch. 2 "The structure of dogmatic statements as an ecumenical problem"; and Austin Farrer, *Faith and Speculation* (A. & C. Black 1967).

[3] E. Stauffer, *New Testament Theology* (S.C.M. Press 1963), note 585 on c.43.

The first article of the Creed requires us to respect a fundamental distinction between God and all that God creates. The subordinate distinctions—heaven and earth, things visible and things invisible—do not have clarity in use which once they had. The varied and vague associations which these verbal signposts have acquired may confuse and hinder the work which has to be done; but I shall try to proceed with the main business of this essay without stopping to put them into use afresh by careful mapwork. Let us proceed with scrupulous respect for the main distinctions : between God and all that God creates, and between the knowledge God has and the knowledge which men acquire experientially. Through God's generosity as Creator, men and their world are what God knows them to be. Men have their own awareness of created actuality and of the agencies involved. Their awareness is ill informed in many respects; it can be better informed if God gives himself to them so that they may share his knowledge. Those who believe that God does precisely this may find it appropriate to say that what men receive as the creatures of God and as his partners in knowledge comes to them by two distinguishable routes : one runs through the matrix of spatio-temporal physicality, and the other supervenes upon that matrix in the experience called "conscience".

Set thus to live, men also are aware that, with their world, they are in pilgrimage; and Christians believe that in this pilgrimage God takes his creatures from "first" and "old" things to "new" and "last" things. This faith informs their will to live. At the heart of Christian tradition lies the convicion that God in his self-giving so relates himself to men that he takes up their wills into his own. Where faith prevails in the tumult of experience, Christian men are able to express their own will in the prayer : Thy will be done on earth as it is in heaven. Through Jesus Christ, author of that prayer wherever it is truly made, faith rests upon God the Creator of heaven and earth. All things are subject to his rightful authority, and in his will is our peace.

One further comment on human habits must be made and then we can get to work. Men, apt to discern what they must deal with and what deals with them, organize their awareness in ways best fitted to serve their rational interest. This organized appreciation is aptly and frequently done by the complementary application of three sets of categorical tools : one which picks out *physical* features, one which picks out *political* features, and one which picks out *personal* features, in the actuality with which (and in which) men must engage.[4] The man of faith, whose will God has taken up into

---

[4] Readers who are inclined to press this distinction into the form of com-pounding reality "naturalistically", "historically", and "aesthetically and

his own, claims to receive into his own knowledge something of the knowledge which God has of him and of his affairs. Paul, as we have noted, does this with particular reference to the invisible future prepared in heaven already, into which the whole creation will move at its final consummation. The three complementary category-sets are prominently in use; for this particular reference fits into a larger persuasion that God, self-expressed in Jesus Christ, is at work in creation, through a process[5] of righteousness in the course of which he overcomes nullifying opposition to his will, to achieve with his creatures a final glory. Physical actualities, affirmed as heaven and earth with mankind housed in them, are subject to political action, which is personal on God's part and evokes personal action from mankind. Within an enterprise of creation, life is being given to men; and "if anyone is in Christ he is a *new* creation; the old has passed away, behold, the new has come" (2 Cor. 5. 17).

With what expectation, reasonably entertained in hope and expressed through love, may the man of faith look forward with questions in his mind about his own physicality and about the physical universe with which he is so deeply involved in the receiving of life? With the divergent languages of apocalypse, of speculative illumination, and of philosophical apologetic, the early Christians tried to do business in this matter. They took seriously the promised access to "secret and hidden wisdom" which "God has revealed to us through the Spirit". For them, as for us, it was debatable whether the "new" and "last", fully deployed, would in any sense incorporate the facts of spatio-temporal physicality given in the "first" actuality of man in his world. An apostolic assertion that "the *form* of this world is passing away" (1 Cor. 7. 31b) is ambiguous in this respect. Its author suggests elsewhere that the whole creation will be taken up in the final consummation and share in the glory of the children of God (Rom. 8. 21; cf. Eph. 1. 10; Col. 1. 20); but would he have denied the predicted annihilation of the material world to which others allude (1 John 2. 17a; Rev. 20. 11 and 21. 1b; 2 Pet. 3. 10f.)?

We cannot, of course, be sure that we know what is being talked about here. Every closed account of spatio-temporal physicality which men give to themselves is liable to be disrupted. But there are facts, not wholly of our making, which provoke real questions. To the man who affirms creation these are facts in which the will of God is expressed; and when God's will is finally accomplished, his

religiously" may of course do so—at some risk. Cf. W. Dantine, "Creation and Redemption", *Scottish Journal of Theology*, vol. 18, no. 2.

[5] The judicial associations of this term should be held in mind.

purpose in so ordering things will, we hope, be transparently plain. Will it be plain as the purpose of a ladder is plain to those who have climbed it and, from the height scaled, see how and why it was placed as it was, with freedom thereafter to discard it? Or will it be plain because in the end materiality for men in a physical universe will serve gloriously (in ways we do not now experience) to mediate the imperishable life which God wills to give to his creatures?[6]

In 2 Peter 1. 2-11 and 3. 2-13, as in Revelation 21. 1-6, the universal framework envisaged for redeemed human lives is unambiguously identified as "new heavens and a new earth". Can we find an appropriate theology which prepares men at any rate to consider what is said in those passages? If the second option about plainness is correct, it will be theology which encourages us to find here a reference to actualities which are not wholly immersed into the activity of rational human agents, as the physical universe of our present experience is not. Those who believe that man's chief and highest end is to glorify God and fully to enjoy him for ever are frequently disposed to treat as fully actual, and to envisage as finally actual, only what is incorporated into the activity of rational agents. If the raw crudities of the physical universe *repel* them, they share with other pessimists the language of gnostic illumination, whose logic is to dissociate the created world from God and to assign to some demiurge the power in physical existence. If, on the other hand, the wonder of the world *holds their admiration*, they try to share with other sensitive admirers the language of philosophical reflection. 2 Peter 1 (notably verse 4 with its reference to becoming "partakers of the divine nature") will provide a principal theological bearing, and it will be the theological language of incarnation and transfiguration whose logic they will most readily explore.

Leaving aside gnostic dualism, let us consider the theology offered by E. L. Mascall. With a sharp eye on the misconception "that Jesus

6 This second possibility is being explored with vigour by theologians from all the main traditions who are concerned that redemption should be affirmed in proper relation to creation. From Lutheranism we hear Wingren insisting that "belief in creation means that we cannot isolate a 'religious' part, our soul, from the rest of us, or separate body from soul on the false assumption that only the soul can have any relationship to God"; "the basic fact that we live constitutes the primary relationship to God" (G. Wingren, *Creation and Law* (Oliver & Boyd 1961), pp. 26f). E. L. Mascall has contributed substantially to the discussion in *The Christian Universe* and in *Theology and the Future* (Darton, Longman & Todd 1966 and 1968) Cf. papers at a colloquium. in 1964—"The New Testament Doctrine of Ktisis", by G. W. H. Lampe in *Scottish Journal of Theology*, vol. 17, no. 4; "Nature", by P. Evdokimov in ibid., vol. 18, no. 1; "Creation and Redemption", by W. Dantine in ibid., vol. 18, no. 2.

Christ is of immense significance to human beings, but of no importance whatever to the rest of the universe",[7] Mascall draws out a theology of "Christification". This theology, as also that of Teilhard whom he cautionsuly invokes,[8] directs attention to the present radiation of grace, overarched by "the reality of the consummated Christ"; but it does not interpret for us the Petrine injunction to "*wait* for new heavens and a new earth in which righteousness dwells". Mascall wishes to take the cosmic symbolism of this text as more than a metaphor. The hope set before us is "that both the human race and the material universe, of which the human race is part, may be taken up into the very life of God himself and be transformed into a condition of unimaginable glory".[9] His theology, like that of Teilhard[10], displays merit for lack of which any theology will be suspect. It maintains the proper reserve which must characterize any human effort to foretell the consummation of God's purposes. It cannot be dismissed as *idle* speculation, for it directs men's will to live into the healing channels of sacramental worship and towards a Christian handling of this world's present business. Its Omega-expectation is shaped by looking down the perspectives offered now to highly cultivated men. The hazards posed by religious language which, in pagan use, purports to divinize what is not divine, are overcome—and the perils of Nature-worship dispelled—by practical theology which points to the consecration of the world in liturgy; and experiences of transfiguration, given in the way of asceticism, come to their own. What, if anything, is missing, when the theology we seek is developed along these lines?

The divergent languages of apocalyticism, gnostic speculation, and philosophical apologetic were all employed in an effort to declare "the unseen" for which empirical languages of natural science and of history are inappropriate (however relevant to the declaration what is said in those languages may be). The particular declaration about new heavens and a new earth was originally made in the language of apocalyptic. Apocalyptic testimony declares the divine enterprise of creation, within which we, with our entire world, derive being from God. It declares that God's creation is distorted by the power which lurks in idolatrous religion and sensualist seduction. It declares that men, with their world, will be

---

[7] *The Christian Universe*, p. 163.
[8] *The Christian Universe*, pp. 91ff, 142ff; *Theology and the Future*, pp. 78ff.
[9] *The Christian Universe*, p. 109.
[10] I have nothing to add, by way of direct discussion of Teilhard, to what others provide. Cf. *The Phenomenon of Man* and *Le Milieu Divin*, and also *An Introduction to Teilhard de Chardin*, by N. M. Williers.

renewed and glorified as God's creation when this process of salvation is accomplished. It elicits confidence in future acts of God which will give life to men and provide a framework serving to sustain that life in imperishable glory. Where this language is used in the New Testament (and we may take 2 Peter 3. 13 and Revelation 21. 1 as the clearest cases), the framework, identified in both cases as "new heavens and a new earth", fills the void left by demolition of the present framework of spatio-temporal physicality. The intention, again in both cases, is that mankind should have the only kind of home in which we know human life to be possible, but should have it in a new and final form where the promise of life in unimpaired fellowship with God is gloriously fulfilled—"in which righteousness dwells" (2 Pet. 3. 13), into which "the new Jerusalem descends" (Rev. 21. 2-4). The passion which carried this thesis into Christian eschatology is something we can share if we read Isaiah 56—65, taking it as sequel to Isaiah 40—55, with the event of Jesus Christ vivid in our experience. Isaiah 65. 17, once absorbed in that discipline of faith seeking understanding, is not easily abandoned: "Behold, I create new heavens and a new earth; and the former things shall not be remembered or come into mind. Be glad and rejoice for ever in that which I create!" "Create", moreover, is a word with rich associations, and a second intention attaches itself to the thesis of new heavens and a new earth: by their establishment, the inherent goodness of all that the Creator has brought into being will at last be fully and publicly displayed.

In this apocalyptic tradition we find Papias declaring that "the kingdom of Christ will be established on this earth σωμάτικος. We have the allusion in Acts 3. 21 to "times of ἀποκαταστάσεως πάντων (reinstatement of all things)". This theme, borrowed from paganism as Lactantius happily points out,[11] construes the Christian hope in a

---

11 *Inst.* VII, c. 18: Of the fortunes of the world at the last time, and of the things foretold by soothsayers.

That these things will thus take place, all the prophets have announced from the inspiration of God, and also the soothsayers at the instigation of the demons. . . . But, withdrawn from their account, not without fraud on the part of the demons, was that the Son of God would then be sent, who, having destroyed all the wicked, would set at liberty the pious. Which, however, Hermes did not conceal. For in that book which is entitled The Complete Treatise, after an enumeration of the evils concerning which we have spoken, he added: "But when these things come to pass, then he who is Lord, and Father, and God, and Creator of the first, and sole God, looking upon what is done, and opposing to the disorder his own will (i.e. goodness), recalling the wandering and cleansing wickedness, and partly inundating it with much water and partly burning it with most rapid fire, and sometimes pressing it with wars and pestilences, *he brought his world to its ancient state and renewed it.*

fashion which speaks to longings widely entertained—though on a falsely cyclic basis—in the Graeco-Roman world. We have, too, the theologies with which Paul, Mark, and Luke mediate to us the Christ-event. If Helmut Flender is right in his recent contribution to our understanding of them, each in his own way distinguishes between the renewal of the old world to its original purpose as God's creation and the eschatological new creation, of which the restored creation, for its limited time, is parabolic.[12]

None of this, one need hardly say, stands in its own right. It rests in faith's response to Jesus Christ: a man in history whose presence bears witness to the authority of God and to his asserting of that authority through process of conflict leading to victory, in the age-long engagement with the enterprise of creation. The manhood of Jesus, from conception to burial, was wrought out in the context of "heaven and earth" which is our own present context. But in his case a unique claim is made about his manhood: that it is now re-expressed in imperishable life, bound as σῶμα πνευμάτικον in in-dissoluble unity with the divine origin of all life. He has passed through death into the world's future; there he is "with God"; and in post-resurrection appearances he has disclosed himself to men living where we now live—an occurrence, or set of occurrences, which throw a question-mark against every closed account of spatio-temporal physicality which men concoct.[13] He has disclosed himself as "the Lord who is to come". In the meantime, he unites our works and ways with the works and ways of God "in the Spirit". By this inaugurated eschatology we are encouraged in faith to taste the powers of the world to come and to live in this world now as men equipped for life in the glory of God's consummated creation.

The will so to live here and now is strengthened and guided by theological explorations which are closely related to the one which immediately concerns us, but are not identical with it.[14] Good work has been done on the theme of "cosmocrats" (falsely divinized authorities of culture) and their subjection to God in Christ. Work has also been done on the implications of this Christology and eschatology for the self-understanding and practice of the Church in its worldly role and service. It must suffice here to note, without

[12] H. Flender, "Das Verständnis der Welt bei Paulus, Markus und Lukas" in *Kerugma und Dogma* (1968), Heft 1.

[13] E. Schlink, "Zum Gespräch des Christlichen Glaubens mit der Naturwissenschaft" in *Medicus Viator* (Tübingen, J. C. B. Mohr, 1959); M. C. Perry, *The Easter Enigma* (Faber 1959).

[14] A. D. Galloway, *The Cosmic Christ*. Nisbet 1951. In Davies and Daube, ed., *The Background of the New Testament and its Eschatology* (Cambridge 1954) there are highly relevant articles: "Christ, Creation and the Church", by N. A. Dahl and "Kerugma, Eschatology and Social Ethics", by A. N. Wilder.

investigating, the possibility that these explorations supply sign-posts which suggest that cosmically the way forward is to a new heavens and a new earth, where physicality in a physical universe (a state which at present seems to be constitutive for manhood) is not abandoned but renewed— renewed by acts of God of which we have had some intimation in advance not only by the post-resurrection appearances of Christ but also by his transfiguration. But sign-posts are not maps. We have no maps. And if we take our bearings from physicality as at present we experience it, we find ourselves wrestling with difficulties which have put a brake on apocalyptic exuberance. Our task is to focus, if we can, an expecta-tion reasonably held in faith and hope, one which bears fruit now in appropriate deeds of love; and it must be done with theological sobriety, a virtue not conspicuously present in apocalyptists, though it is worth remembering that theological exhilaration is not to be equated with theological intoxication and primly repudiated![15]

With brakes gently applied, philosophical theologians have turned into other linguistic territories where difficulties about physicality have sometimes brought them near to dissolving redemptive history into timeless myth. We need not follow those who strayed into the language of speculative illumination. The Church's resistance to Gnostics "who tried to dissociate the created world from God, in order to assign to the demiurge the power in physical and external existence"[16] is enshrined in the first article of the Creed. Notoriously there was not, and still is not, a comparable resistance to the tempta-tions offered through the language of philosophical apologetic, which, in varying forms, expresses "an attitude to life which is defined by the ideal of the development of personality". These temptations, particularly as presented in traditions stemming from Platonist "idealism", have been kept under critical scrutiny, but not always to everyone's satisfaction.[17] Good men and true have always been ready to argue that both alternatives to the language of apocalypticism evoke theological reports on God's works and ways with his world which are insufficiently *theocratic* to satisfy the

---

[15] G. B. Caird, *Commentary on the Revelation of St John the Divine* (A. & C. Black 1966) provides an impressive and timely exposition of the religious and intellectual power in that piece of apocalyptic.

[16] G. Wingren, *Creation and Law*, p. 4.

[17] In Davies and Daube, ed., *Background*, "Eschatologie biblique et idealisme platonicien", by J. Héring. Three more recent works provide very rewarding guidance: H. Chadwick, *Early Christian Thought and the Classical Tradition* (O.U.P. 1966); R. A. Norris, *God and World in Early Christian Theology* (A. & C. Black 1966); Angelo P. O'Hagan, *Material recreation in the Apostolic Fathers* (Akademie-Verlag Berlin).

Christian conscience. Be that as it may, the difficulties which men have in reconciling spatio-temporal physicality with final glory must not be evaded.

Spatio-temporal physicality, taken abstractly as a *form* of creaturely being, does not present difficulty in principle for theistic religion. It is a form appropriate to finitude; one in which creatures evidently *hold their own* and exert their God-given *power* to be. Taken materially, as matter of fact, it is riddled with suggestions of ultimate recalcitrance to the grace we look for in the works and ways of God. The suggestions fall under two broad heads, roughly corresponding to two grounds of opposition which Paul diagnosed in the resistance put up to his preaching of Christ crucified, the power of God and the wisdom of God. Men reared in Judaism put up religious opposition; Gentiles put up rational opposition; both had to be "called" out of their habitual attitudes to a fresh apprehension of grace.

Man's own physicality, and the dominant constituents in his physical environment, attract from him a confidence which easily passes into worship; and worship is rightly to be given only to God. Where men's will to live is corrupted by misplaced worship, God's enterprise of creation is distorted, not only in manhood itself but in everything with which men have dealings. Early theologians, whilst resisting the Gnostics' radical mistrust of physical actuality, vehemently contested all tendencies to assume that material principles are ultimate. "The heart of the matter for Clement always lies in the doctrine of the transcendent Creator upon whose will and providence the created order is dependent and with whom this world is in no sense identical".[18] Philosophical theologians stood with apocalyptists in repudiating the power which lurks in sensualist seduction and in the refinements of idolatry to which it leads. But, asks the religious man, can actualities which serve so to seduce men be glorified in the final triumph of God's purposes?

The universe in all its physical actuality so imposes itself upon men that their effort to live is marred, to the eye of faith, by evidence of opposition to God. Where, however, is the principle of opposition properly to be located? The Gnostics had their unacceptable answer in a dualism which denied Christian belief in creation. If the principle is not to be traced to God himself, an alternative is to locate it solely in man's perverse will; but this is perhaps unduly presumptuous, and does not in any case remove

18 H. Chadwick, op. cit., p. 46.

theological difficulties about the goodness of the Creator's work. The evidence, moreover, is that evil is inflicted upon men from the non-human environment in ways which cannot be exhaustively covered by tracing the evil men impose on the environment. Karl Barth has tried to safeguard what is at stake in formulation of the thesis that the relationship between Creator and creature is disrupted by a nullifying element "which is compatible with neither the goodness of the Creator nor that of the creature, and which cannot be derived from either side but can only be regarded as hostility in relation to both".[19] With consistent stress on the negativity of all that comes into view, and with careful attention to appropriate distinctions, he succeeds to my mind in providing a report on God's process against evil which opens the way to a religiously tolerable hope of redemption for all that God has created, by reconciliation and renewal.

A prospect of cleansing from corruption and of liberation from distortion does not, however, necessarily suffice for minds troubled in another way about physicality. Those most troubled in this other way are men whose will to live has for its spearhead the power of intellect; men who often invite the description "rootless cosmopolitans and aristocrats of the mind". Aristocrats of the mind are unwilling to be comfortably or uncomfortably at home along with the world's minerals, vegetables, and animals. They want to *know*. Physicality being as it is, their aspiration to succeed through knowing lies under threat.[20] The difficulties posed by finitude and by death are not, perhaps, insuperable; nor are those posed by the immensity and complexity of physical fact or by the dangers in physical power. The threat arises from the strong hint that what is physical is, in the last resort, opaque and therefore ultimately intractable to the rational agency of mind. One way of repelling this threat is to affirm the superiority of rational agency to physical functioning and in the end to write off whatever is not subsumed into that superior agency.

---

[19] K. Barth, *Church Dogmatics III*, 3 (T. & T. Clark 1960), c. 50, 1—"The Creator and his Creation".

[20] A. D. Galloway (*The Cosmic Christ*) is an excellent guide to the varying ways in which men have shown awareness of this threat. Dr Galloway's own —modern—way of putting it is that the not-self, in its physicality, seems to be an impersonal intrusion upon personal life. On pp. 150-3 he cites two passages, one from a second-century Gnostic and the other from Kant, each of which "expresses fear, awe, and a feeling of insignificance in the face of the vast, uncontrollable, impersonal forces of nature. Each expresses this in a different way, but to both such a universe appears to be ultimately incompatible with the fulfilment of personal life." The question raised is therefore: By what redemptive act of God is personal life in an impersonal universe fulfilled in such a way that all experience becomes an encounter with God?

The threat is repelled but not finally dispelled. Perhaps, after all, it should not be dispelled but rather absorbed into a will to live which is transmuted into the richer way of love.

It is consistent for aristocrats of the mind to hope that in the end men will be liberated from every trace of physicality, so that rational agents, eternally preserved, lie open to one another and to God unencumbered by the "otherness" which physicality secures for whatever displays it, including men themselves. Now all who have discovered that men live by love for what is other than themselves will find some attraction in this hope; for love is served by knowledge. An aspiration for life in which love is *transcended* by knowledge probably reflects a distortion of humanity, and a disposition towards living as a rootless cosmopolitan may be a still greater distortion; but the protest against perpetual "otherness" which lies somewhere near the root of an intellectual aversion from physicality is not to be lightly dimissed. Yet, if life can be construed in terms of love, which is served but not transcended by knowledge; and if love presupposes "otherness" which it overcomes without destroying; then it is reasonable to contemplate a consummation in which, together with God and men, creatures other than men have their part.

Traditionally this contemplation has been unfolded in thought-patterns with pyramid structure and an hierarchical system of subordination. By virtue of the Son's subjecting of all creatures to himself, and in virtue of his own subjection to the Father, God "will be everything to everything" (1 Cor. 15. 28). The pyramid is filled out by adding the thesis that non-human creatures have their place in the final glory by subjection to mankind. We do not know how to admit this thesis without arrogance; and modern man's modest estimate of hs own importance in his newly seen universe provides (where it exists) a salutary echo of the warning against arrogance which Christians must listen to from another and decisive source. Men are not fit to speak about the commission given to them to "fill the earth and subdue it, and have dominion over every living thing that moves upon it", nor to act upon that commission, until the judgement of God on human pride and human hardness has been carried home. It is carried home proleptically in faith broken and remade before the cross and the empty tomb of Jesus. It will be finally carried home in death and in that to which death is the gateway. Any prospect we may hold of an "earth", given afresh to the children of men, with its "heavens", must be seen under the discipline of God's judgement on mankind. Such a prospect, and the hope which goes with it for power and joy in living, are subject to the grace in which God gives himself to free our race from its guilt.

If, then, we affirm our hope, in faith which already leaps to lose its chains, we should do so with modest reserve about man's dominion and let the emphasis rest on the glory which God will create when nothing obstructs his will.[21]

In the present inglorious state of affairs we cannot affirm that God is everything to everything. Idolized creatures and idolizing men offer the plainest evidence against any such affirmation, and what nullifies it at this centre is operative wherever we look. That the good creatures of God are everywhere drawing their life from God must be affirmed in faith; but the life so drawn is not being returned to him in gratitude, only to be enjoyed afresh in the glad exchange of love. Physical actuality *as we experience it* obstructs the consummation of creation in a glory so envisaged. God, so we may affirm, is rightly at work in judgement to demolish it, and by dying we too shall be engulfed in that demolition. But the final word about God's creation of mankind as physical beings in a physical universe rests with God. It is a word already uttered in the inaugurated eschatology from which Christians take their bearings. The possibility that demolishing judgement is God's final word is ruled out by the presence, in this inaugurated eschatology, of resurrection from the dead, and indeed of transfiguration as a present possibility (Mark 9. 2 and parallels; 1 Cor. 15. 51). The cosmic hopes expressed in Romans 8. 21, in Ephesians 1. 10, in Colossians 1. 20, and spelt out in the apocalyptic passages which have claimed our special attention, must be maintained in fidelity to God.

Throughout this paper I have deliberately used the Greek forms (derived from φύσις) of the words traditionally used to characterize spatio-temporal actuality and have avoided the Latin derivates, "natural" and "material". I will not argue the case for doing so here. It is, I believe, likely that these Latin terms have acquired associations which confuse and obscure what is under discussion. The problem is to find and to use a language which will serve to reflect

[21] Cf. E. Schlink (*The Coming Christ and the Coming Church*, pp. 62f), where "The Basic Forms of Human Perception" are under discussion, the pyramidal one having been introduced on p .56.

The thought-form of a pyramid with its hierarchical system of subordination does not succeed in comprehending the relationship between God and the world, because God meets the world in Christ as the wholly other Lord—wholly other not only in his omnipotence, but also because He, the Most High, has come down to us in Christ as the humblest of all.

K. Heim's discussion of The World's Perfector, in Part Three of *Jesus the World's Perfector* (Oliver & Boyd 1959) introduces all the insights which impose theological reserve.

in our own awareness the knowledge we believe God to have about us and our affairs. It must, I suggest, be language which catches up spatio-temporal physicality into the enterprise of "world-making" which is also "history-making": language which does this by referring to *creation*, to a *process* of righteousness, to glorious *fulfilment* of will and purpose. Language of this kind has been made available for theological use from the experience of a civic community—"founded", "defended, ruled and rectified", consolidated after episodes of critical strain with ceremonial "triumph". The peace of any such *civis* depends on the rightful authority under which it lives and on the grace and power of that authority's actual operation. When borrowed for theological use, to portray the rightful authority of God over all that is, the term *spirit* is employed to indicate by what agency God's will takes effect with grace and power. This name, alas, has been used so diversely and so loosely that we hesitate about doing further business with it. But if we abandon it the lacuna is not easily filled.

"The Spirit of God is the concept for the activity of the one and only God in history and creation. It can serve as a direct expression for God's inner being and for his present reality."[22] "Spirit" is a word which points beyond the physical to what transcends it but at the same time impinges upon it under two aspects. First, it impinges as the operation of divine authority, expressed as will, potent for salvation or destruction. Secondly, it impinges as the intrinsic power of God to give being and life from himself to another and to receive such another into his own life. It is by Spirit that God promises to be everything to everything, when what is created (as "flesh"), and corrupted by sin but judged and rectified, is finally established as the creature wholly plastic to his will; something which by his free decision he will *own* for ever as his glory.

There are discrepancies in the use of this language, associated with different branches of theological tradition, and it is difficult to track down their sources. Theologians whose habits have been formed within one branch and who try to move out into larger ecumenical freedom have not yet come together in newly confident speech. Some light has been thrown on the problems for me in an article by J. Meyendorff, from which I cite the paragraph most relevant to my own initial habits:

The development followed by Barth in his later works and leading to a new discovery of the Word of God in the created world, to a solidarity between God and man in the natural order—this idea was

---

22 Kittel, TWNT—*pneuma*. Cf. E. Schweitzer, etc., *Spirit of God* (A. & C. Black 1960), p. 5.

always strong in the West, both in Thomism and in modern liberalism, and was also stressed by Russian sophiologists—is still quite different from the notion of a supernatural mutual participation of God and man in the Church, through the Word's historic incarnation.[23]

Is this difference generated, in part at least, by the suspect associations of "natural/supernatural" terminology; or does it go back to insufficiently criticized presuppositions about the relations in which God, mankind, and the world are deemed to be? From Lutheranism we have Wingren's summons to take our presuppositions more simply from the Old Testament:

> The Old Testament describes a humanity which has been created by God, and which, represented by the peculiar people of God who had been chosen for the salvation of the whole of the human race, could do no more than await the outpouring of the Spirit. The humanity which awaits the Spirit, created by God and subject to the discipline of the Law, is the same humanity into which the Spirit comes in the present time through the Gospel and the Church.[24]

Theological language is Church language. "In the Church we live under the constraint of the Holy Spirit; we know the grace of God in Jesus Christ and trust it as sufficient for the redemption of men and women in all their need; our lives are exposed to the claim of God and we learn about his will for human beings both before and after death."[25] What affirmations are we entitled to make about the physical universe?

God exerts his will to give life to creatures; through physical and historical process he rules against the principle of enmity which threatens to nullify his will; at the end he will establish what he has created in the glory of divine ownership. He has done all this already with the man upon whom the process of righteousness was concentrated. Will he not, with him, freely give us all things? Has he not already assured us that this will be so "through the Spirit"?

It is still debatable whether the "new" and "last", fully deployed, will incorporate the facts of spatio-temporal physicality given as our universe in the "first" actualizing of creation and maintained throughout the process of creation but doomed to demolition as all men are doomed to death. Is it in order to suppose that after the impending demolition—and, for the human individual, after death —these physicalities will have served their turn and can be reckoned

---

[23] J. Meyendorff, "The Significance of the Reformation in the History of Christendom" in the *Ecumenical Review*, vol. xvi (January 1964), p. 177.
[24] G. Wingren, *Creation and Law*, p. 16.
[25] *A Declaration of Faith* (Congregational Church in England & Wales), preamble, p. 8.

with an "old" which has passed away? Is there any secret and hidden wisdom for us which God has revealed through the Spirit? Our modern distaste for mystery-mongering, and sceptical detachment from the biblical presentation of God's enterprise in creation, prompt in us the reply : we do not know—and why should we care? Why, indeed, should men include within things hoped for a universe which is neither God nor their fellow men? Such a universe is theirs at present. It has features strongly suggesting that it is there in many respects for its own sake and not just for ours; nor are these features wholly ascribable to a present enslavement under sin, distorting mankind and all that mankind must deal with. It defies, and threatens to defeat, our capacity for love. Such a universe, however it be glorified, threatens to be "an impersonal intrusion upon personal life". There now, it serves in many ways to excite and sustain men's will to live; but it is the proximate cause of defeat for that will.

All Christian hope rests in one who is not defeated by what defeats men. It looks to the God of grace who will give himself to men, dealing first with their guilt and then with the debility and corruption which weaken their creaturely power to be. The hope is that God will take men through death and final judgement and then renew them in power for a life of glory, where all experience will be participation in God's own joy. Does this presuppose a framework of which our present physical universe is parabolic? Moved by respect for God's present works and ways in the act of life-giving, I am inclined to believe that God's answer to that question will be yes! How, otherwise, will life for *men* be given to us? How, otherwise, shall we exert the power of human life?

This essay began with prolegomena evoked by the shade of Immanuel Kant. It turns back to him in a postscript where I will borrow references from Peter Baelz to Kant.[26]

> Whatever else he is, man is a child of nature and part of the natural world. He is to a large degree what he is because nature is what it is. Thus the metaphysical questions concern not simply the meanings he can give to his own life, but the meaning which life can give to him (p. 32).

Reflecting on what he knows most intimately, man begins with himself, an agent acting with knowledge formed in categories of causal explanation. Man does not create all that he experiences as a subject; he is not God. His reflections are halted at frontiers of agnosticism which Kant located in his own way :

26 P. Baelz, *Christian Theology and Metaphysics* (Epworth Press 1968), pp. 32ff.

The justification of our right to expect the external world to conform to our causal categories of explanation is accompanied by the assertion that we had no right to expect those categories to apply *beyond* the external world. They were restricted in their range to the world of space and time as it must appear to man; they could not be extended beyond the phenomenal world to whatever existed in itself apart from its appearance to man (p. 34).

But man's worldliness "threatens to destroy his status as a rational, moral being. This threat can be held at bay only if his worldliness is in the last resort subordinated to his moral rationality" (p. 38). In Kant's analysis the postulate of God is inextricably linked with this assertion of ontological priority for man's moral rationality over whatever is phenomenally apparent.

We are now, and not for the first time, dealing within a physical universe which threatens so to impose itself as to crowd out man's coveted self-esteem and to deprive his appeals to God of the weight they have been thought to carry. Theses marked by anthropocentric claims must be advanced, if at all, against critical resistance; and so, though not in consequence, must theses marked by theocentric postulates. What Eliade has called "the anxiety of man living in Time" is a fertile womb of myths, dreams, and mysteries which must not be admitted without close scrutiny into the texture of reasonable faith. The most admissible among these at present is

> that most important mythological tradition of the modern world, which can be said to have had its origin with the Greeks, to have come of age in the Renaissance, and to be flourishing today in continuous healthy growth, in the works of those artists, poets, and philosophers of the West for whom the wonder of the world itself— as it is now being analysed by science—is the ultimate revelation.[27]

If, as seems plausible, Heidegger stands to the twentieth-century European mind as Kant stood to that mind in his day, we must take seriously Heidegger's question about what it means "to be in the world", not only as mind but as concrete being. We must share too his determination to take seriously the φύσις with which beings become and remain observable: an "opening-up and inward-jutting-beyond-itself", declaring a power to be and a right to be which aristocrats of the mind must not lightly brush off. Heidegger, nevertheless, is an aristocrat of the mind who has picked up the Idealist torch and tried to carry some of its light into our own century. There is mystery in φύσις, not exhausted in our scientific dealings with physical things. "The Greeks did not learn what φύσις is through natural phenomena, but the other way round; it was

[27] Joseph Campbell, *The Masks of God*, vol. 1 (Secker & Warburg 1959), p. 7.

through a fundamental poetic and intellectual experience of being
that they discovered what they had to call φύσις".[28] Yet Heidegger
can also be described as the grave-digger of German Idealism: an
Idealism "rooted in the Mediator, in reconciliation in history, in the
Golden Age".

> Heidegger knows no Mediator but poetry. Heidegger knows no world
> but the material one in which he attempts to find meaning and
> reconciliation. . . . Heidegger destroys the Idealist reconciliation of
> the spiritual and material worlds as revealing each other, through
> faith for Bengel or reason for Hegel".[29]

Through Heidegger's torch-bearing and grave-digging hands we
inherit

> the poetical and religious visions of a universe hidden by Satan but at
> the same time revealing the Light (Being). Heidegger is deeply
> immersed in the Nothing (Satan) as the veiling of Being (Light), in the
> anxiety, deepened by the shocking realization of demonic possibilities,
> lying at the root of earthly reality. Salvation may lie in the poetically
> lived existence.[30]

For what poetically lived existence have men been set free in
Christian faith? In their inner freedom from guilt and in their
outward activities of service, in tokens of blessing which lead
Cullmann to write about the proleptic deliverance of the body, and
others too to write about proleptic dominion in grace over the rest
of creation, Christian men have in their faith the gift of life at its
best, to be enjoyed here and now in worldly circumstances and to be
celebrated for the witness it bears to what is to come. Present
victories over illness and promised victory even over death, enacted
with and for the body; dethroning of all cosmocrats—false authorities lording it over human culture; union for men with their Saviour
in subjection to the Father; prospects, however enigmatic, of
glorified physicality with God everything to everything—all this,
we want to say, comes to us now from the future in the Spirit. It
does not come as a matter of course. It comes, in a world "charged
with the grandeur of God", through hints and tokens which "flame
out, like shining from shook foil".[31]

Whilst we still live on this side of the judgement into which we
shall be plunged by death, we do not see what God has prepared for

[28] M. Heidegger, *An Introduction to Metaphysics* (Doubleday, Anchor edn
1961), p. 12.
[29] M. Heidegger, *The Question of Being* (Vision 1959), pp. 9-10 from the
preface by W. Klubach and J. T. Wilde.
[30] Ibid.
[31] Gerard Manley Hopkins, *Poems* (O.U.P. 1930), p. 26.

those who love him. We play our part in world-making, in history-making, under conditions of spatio-temporal physicality which conceal the limit which embraces them and pose death as the final absurdity. The order of physical reality reflects some radiance of wisdom and love; it reflects, too, the pride and the hardness with which God is opposed. It invites demolition—and it invites restoration in free grace. Faith cannot satisfactorily state in prose what man is not yet able to see. But it is not disreputable for faith to find expression in prayer and praise—and to sing its belief in poetry as the liturgical counterpoint to the concrete obedience of poetic living. Faith finds expression in liturgical worship even among Welsh (and English) nonconformists:

> Thy love is the bond of creation,
> Thy love is the peace of mankind.
> Make safe with thy love every nation
> In concord of heart and of mind.
> Thy pity alone can deliver
> The earth from her sorrows, dear Lord;
> Her pride and her hardness forgive her,
> Thy blood for her ransom was poured.
> Thy throne, O Redeemer, be founded
> In radiance of wisdom and love;
> Thy name through the wide world be sounded
> Till earth be as heaven above.
> Though hills and high mountains should tremble,
> Though all that is seen melt away,
> Thy voice shall in triumph assemble
> Thy loved ones at dawning of day.[32]

---

[32] Howell Elvet Lewis, *Congregational Praise*, No. 342.

theological collections 13

Eschatology is no longer seen as a marginal problem of theology, but as the basis on which everything in Christian tradition is built. Five of these essays are concerned with various aspects, biblical, theological, and philosophical, of the Christian hope: the editor of Marxism Today contributes a complementary paper on "The Marxist Hope". All were originally delivered at the 1969 conference of the Society for the Study of Theology.

SBN 281 02352 2

£1   20s   net